WE'RE IN BUSINESS

English for commercial practice
and international trade

Students' Book

Susan Norman

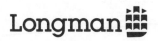

Longman Group UK Limited
*Longman House, Burnt Mill, Harlow,
Essex CM20 2JE, England
and Associated Companies throughout the world*

First published 1983
Sixteenth impression 1994

ISBN 0-582-74872-0

Set in Monophoto 2000 10/11½pt Souvenir Light

Produced by Longman Singapore Publishers Pte Ltd.
Printed in Singapore.

**This book is dedicated to my mothers:
Nanette, Elizabeth and Violet**

Acknowledgements
The author would like to thank the following people for their help in the preparation of this book:
Carolyn de la Plain, once again, for her typing; my husband JLN for all his ideas; Michael Reed
and Eric Mason of Lep and Peter Long for their factual input (all factual errors, of course, I claim
as my own); Delia Greenall, David Cobb, Howard Middle, Sandie Rolfe, Carole Bennett and all the
other people at Longman who helped make this book possible; various friends, relatives and
acquaintances for the use of their names (the characters in this book are entirely fictional and bear
no resemblance to anyone known to me); and all those teachers and students, particularly in Italy,
who have worked through this material with me.   SN

We are grateful to the following for permission to use copyright material:
American Express Company for page 65 (right); Barclays Bank PLC for page 65 (left);
British Airways for pages 47 and 91; Lloyd's of London for pages 29 (middle right and
bottom left), and 35; Longman Photographic Library for pages 80, 81 and 126; Mary
Evans Picture Library for page 29 (middle left and bottom right).

All other photographs by Peter Lake.

Our special thanks to Scurfield of Harlow and Introsound Ltd., of Bishops Stortford, for
the use of their premises on pages 10 and 12,

Illustrators: Oxprint, David Parkins, Paul Crompton.
Cover illustration by Steve Pickard.

Contents 90/u/4

Introduction

Contents

v

Contents

Unit One
Introducing Transworld

 Anne Bell works in the Manchester office of Transworld Freight. She is in the canteen talking to a new employee.

1
Hello. My name's Anne Bell.

Pleased to meet you, Miss Bell. I'm David Thompson.

2
Have you met anyone else yet?

Only Liz, who works in the accounts department with me.

3
Well, the good-looking one over there is Kevin Hughes.

4
Who's he talking to?

That's Jane Long.

5
The young man sitting at the table is Nick Dawson.

6
Let me introduce you to Sandra Parr. Sandra, this is David Thompson. David, this is Sandra.

Hello, Sandra.

Unit 1

Exercise 1.1   *Listening comprehension*

Listen to the tape once through. Then look at these lists and see if you can remember which person at Transworld did what.

1	Anne Bell	a	She did the photocopying.
2	Sandra Parr	b	He ate a sandwich.
3	David Thompson	c	He arranged exports.
4	Liz Shepherd	d	She did the filing.
5	Nick Dawson	e	He spent time at the docks and the airport.
6	Kevin Hughes	f	She took shorthand and typed letters.
7	Jane Long	g	She worked in the accounts department.
		h	She introduced David to Sandra.
		i	He drank a cup of coffee.
		j	He sat at a table.
		k	She welcomed David to Transworld.
		l	He sent customers their bills.
		m	He worked with the customs officials.
		n	He talked to Jane.
		o	She handled airfreight.
		p	He dealt with customers' accounts.

> *Laboratory drill*
> P: Do   R: *Did*

Exercise 1.2   *Present simple and present progressive*

In pairs, discuss your answers to Exercise 1.1 in the present, like this:

P: *What does Anne do?*   R: *She takes shorthand.*
P: *What else does she do?*   R: *She types letters.*
P: *What's Nick doing in the picture?* R: *He's sitting at a table.*
P: *What else is he doing?*   R: *He's eating a sandwich.*

> *Laboratory drill A*
> P: Nick's sitting at a table.   R: *Oh? What's he doing exactly?*
>   He's typing a letter.
> P: Sandra works in reception.   R: *Oh? What does she do exactly?*
>
> *Laboratory drill B*
> P: She handled airfreight.   R: *She handles airfreight.*
>
> *Laboratory drill C*
> P: He sat at a table.   R: *At the moment he's sitting at a table.*

Exercise 1.3   *Job advertisements*

These job advertisements have all been in the newspaper advertising jobs at Transworld. Decide which of the people in Exercise 1.1 has which job and write a sentence about each, like this:

Anne Bell is a secretary.

Busy freight forwarder needs PERSON FRIDAY. Duties to include typing, photocopying, filing and answering phone. Ring 061–8537272

CUSTOMS CLERK required. Experience and good knowledge of customs procedures essential. Good salary. Write to Transworld Freight plc, 74 Dockside, Manchester M15 7BJ

Our freight forwarding business is expanding and we need an experienced **Airfreight Clerk** to handle our growing airfreight business. Call 8537272

SECRETARY WANTED. Can you type, take shorthand and use a PMBX switchboard? Can you organise a small friendly office? Then ring 061-8537272. We have a job for you.

JUNIOR ACCOUNTS CLERK needed to handle customer accounts in freight forwarders. Good pay. Ring 061–8537272

Senior Accounts Clerk to be in charge of accounts dept in Manchester branch of freight forwarders. Contact Transworld Freight plc, 74 Dockside, Manchester M15 7BJ Tel: 061–8537272

TRANSWORLD FREIGHT requires EXPORT MANAGER to fill new position and control the export side of our business. Write for an application form to Mr G Davis (Asst Mngr), Transworld Freight plc, 74 Dockside, Manchester M15 7BJ

Exercise 1.4 *Synonyms*

Match the words on the left with the word on the right that means the same. All the words are in the advertisements in Exercise 1.3.

1	need	a	grow
2	expand	b	be in charge of
3	deal with	c	write to or telephone
4	contact	d	require
5	control	e	ring
6	call	f	handle

Exercise 1.5 *Transworld*

What do you know about Transworld? Work in small groups and share the information you remember from Exercises 1.1 to 1.4.

This is some of the work they do:

1   They bring goods into the country.
2   They send goods from one place to another.
3   They pay money to the government for bringing goods into the country.
4   They send goods by air.
5   They send goods by sea.
6   They prepare papers, forms and documents.
7   They send goods out of the country.

Find seven words in the puzzle to say these sentences in other ways,

eg They arrange   i . . .
        handle   t . . .
        deal with   c . . . payments.
                      a . . .
                      s . . .
                      d . . .
                      e . . .

Each number in the puzzle always stands for the same letter. In this puzzle 1 = E.

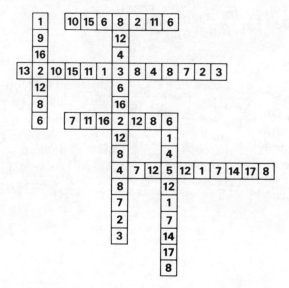

Exercise 1.6   *The alphabet (pronunciation)*

Listen to the tape and write down the twelve groups of four letters you hear, like this:

1   *B O C J*
2   *F B B D*

Laboratory drill	
P: Customs	R: *CUSTOMS*

Exercise 1.7   *Greetings and introductions*

Two short conversations are mixed up together. One is formal and the other is informal.
You are given the first and last line of each dialogue. Put the other lines in the right
order in the right dialogue and decide who is saying each line:

Informal dialogue – First line: 1 *John. It's lovely to see you.*
                    Last line: 7 *Hello, Penny. Nice to meet you.*

Formal dialogue – First line: 8 *Good afternoon. Can I help you?*
                    Last line: 14 *How do you do, Miss Brown.*

  2   John, meet Penny. Penny, this is John.
  3   How do you do, Mr Jones. I'm Susan Smith.
  4   Hello, John.
  5   Fine thanks. And you?
  6   Good afternoon. My name's John Jones.
  9   Hello, Susan. How are you?
10   Mr Jones, I'd like you to meet Miss Brown. Miss Brown, this is Mr Jones.
11   How do you do, Mrs Smith.
12   I'm fine.
13   I'm pleased to meet you, Mr Jones.

Exercise 1.8   *Greeting and introducing people*

On one piece of paper write your first name (eg *Susan*). On another piece of paper write
your title and surname (eg *Mrs Norman*).
Move around the class, sometimes holding up your first name and sometimes holding up
your title and surname.
Greet other people in the class. If they are holding up their first name, greet them
informally. If they are holding up their surname, greet them formally. Introduce other
people to one another, either formally or informally.

Exercise 1.9   *Requests*

In pairs, make requests and reply, like this:

Send a price list   P: *Could you send a price list please?*
                       R: *I'll send it* { *at once.*
                                    { *immediately.*

1   Reply as soon as possible
2   Ring Mr Andrews
3   Photocopy the report
4   Type the memo
5   File the correspondence
6   Answer the letter

Laboratory drill A
P: Could you send a price list please?   R: *I'll send it at once.*

Laboratory drill B
P: Send a price list   R: *Could you send a price list please?*

Exercise 1.10   *Telephone enquiries*

Listen to the tape and fill in the missing words in this telephone conversation:

Transworld: *Transworld. Can I help you?*

Caller: ¹ . . . . . . *I saw your* ² . . . . . *for a junior accounts clerk in this morning's paper.*

T: *Oh yes.*

C: ³ . . . . . *to apply for the* ⁴ . . . . . . ⁵ . . . . . *send me an application form please?*

T: *Certainly.*

C: *And could you tell me* ⁶ . . . . . *about* ⁷ . . . . . .*?*

T: *I'll send details of the job and* ⁸ . . . . . *with the application form.*

C: *Thank you very much.* ⁹ . . . . . *from you* ¹⁰ . . . . . *then.* ¹¹ . . . . .

T: *Just a moment. Could you tell me your name and address?*

C: *Oh yes. It's Andrew* . . . .

Exercise 1.11   *Guided dialogue*

In pairs, pretend to telephone for an application form for the secretary's job in the advertisement in Exercise 1.3. One student is the caller and the other the Transworld switchboard. Then change roles so that the second student telephones about the airfreight clerk's job.

Exercise 1.12   *Business letter terminology*

The words underlined in this letter are the written equivalent of the words you completed in the telephone dialogue in Exercise 1.10. Which words correspond to which?

---

                                                30 Empire Drive
                                                Manchester M6 2PQ

Mr Graham Davis
Assistant Manager
Transworld Freight plc
74 Dockside
Manchester M15 7BJ   8 March 1983

<u>Dear Mr Davis</u>

I saw your <u>advertisement</u> for an Export Manager in the
Daily Herald of 7 March and <u>I would like</u> to apply for
the <u>position.</u>

<u>I would be grateful if you could</u> send me an application
form and <u>further information</u> about the <u>salary</u> and
<u>working conditions.</u>

<u>I look forward to hearing</u> from you in <u>the near future.</u>

<u>Yours sincerely</u>

Geoffrey Andrews

Geoffrey Andrews(Mr)

Exercise 1.13   *Formal written style*

Rewrite these sentences as you would write them in a more formal business letter.

1 I'll expect to see you next week.
2 Could you give me some information about the job?
3 Could you send me your price list?
4 I'll expect to receive the application form soon.
5 Could you see me this week?
6 I'll expect to meet you at the conference.

Exercise 1.14   *A letter of enquiry*

Write a letter of enquiry about the job of Senior Accounts Clerk in the advertisement in Exercise 1.3. Use the same format and business letter conventions as in Exercise 1.12.

Language notes

Pronunciation of the alphabet

a /ei/	b /bi:/	f /ɛf/	i /aɪ/	o /au/	r /a:/	q /kju:/
h /eitʃ/	c /si:/	l /ɛl/	y /waɪ/			u /ju:/
j /dʒei/	d /di:/	m /ɛm/				w /dʌbəlju:/
k /kei/	e /i:/	n /ɛn/				
	g /dʒi:/	s /ɛs/				
	p /pi:/	z /zɛd:/ (UK)				
	t /ti:/					
	v /vi:/					
	z /zi:/ (US)					

Present simple tense

We use the present simple for things we do regularly, always, sometimes, every day etc.

POSITIVE
I/you/we/they work in Manchester.
He/she/it goes through here every day.

The question, short answer and negative are made with the present tense of *to do*.

QUESTION
Does he work?
They work here, don't they?
Where do you work?

SHORT ANSWER
Yes he does/No he doesn't
Yes they do/No they don't

NEGATIVE
I don't work. (I do not work.)
He doesn't work (He does not work.)

Unit 1

Present progressive tense (also called *present continuous tense*)

We use the present progressive to talk about things which are happening while we are talking or which are happening in a picture.

POSITIVE
I am typing (I'm typing)
You are eating (You're eating)
S/he is going (S/he's going)
We are writing (We're writing)
They are meeting (They're meeting)

NEGATIVE
I am not typing (I'm not)
You are not eating (You're not/You aren't)
(He's not/He isn't)
(We're not/We aren't)
(They're not/They aren't)

QUESTION
Is she talking?
You're coming, aren't you?
Where are you going?

SHORT ANSWER
Yes she is/No she isn't (No she's not)
Yes I am/No I'm not

The future: WILL

We use the *will* future when we make a decision at that moment about the future.

I/you/he/she/it/we/they will go

(I'll, he'll, they'll go)

QUESTION
Will you go?
He'll go, won't he?
Where will you work?

SHORT ANSWER
Yes I will. No I won't.
Yes he will. No he won't.

NEGATIVE
I will not do it.   (I won't do it)
He will not come.   (He won't come)

Past simple tense

We use the past simple tense to tell stories about the past. We also use it when the time something happened in the past is known or important.

POSITIVE (regular verbs)
I/you/he/she/it/we/they worked in Manchester from 1978 to 1982.
The question, short answer and negative are made with the past tense of the verb *to do.*

QUESTION
Did you type it yesterday?
He made it, didn't he?
Where did he go on Monday?

SHORT ANSWER
Yes I did. No I didn't.
Yes he did. No he didn't.

NEGATIVE
I didn't do it.
He didn't make it.

See also the list of irregular verbs below and on page 138.

Irregular verbs in this unit

INFINITIVE (present)	PAST SIMPLE	PAST PARTICIPLE
be (am/is/are)	*was/were*	*been*
bring	*brought*	*brought*
deal	*dealt*	*dealt*
do	*did*	*done*
drink	*drank*	*drunk*
eat	*ate*	*eaten*
get	*got*	*got (US gotten)*
give	*gave*	*given*

grow	grew	grown
have/has	had	had
hear	heard	heard
know	knew	known
make	made	made
meet	met	met
pay	paid	paid
put	put	put
ring	rang	rung
say	said	said
see	saw	seen
send	sent	sent
sit	sat	sat
spell	spelt (UK)	spelt (UK)
	spelled (US)	spelled (US)
spend	spent	spent
take	took	taken
tell	told	told
write	wrote	written

British English	American English
Clerk is pronounced /klɑːk/ *Advertisement* is pronounced /ædˈvɛtismənt/	*Clerk* is pronounced /klɛrk/ *Advertisement* is pronounced /ædvərˈtaizmənt/

Business letter format and conventions

Notice the following points:

WRITER'S ADDRESS OR COMPANY LETTERHEAD: at the top or in the top right-hand corner. The writer's name is not at the top of the letter.

READER'S NAME, POSITION AND ADDRESS: on the left. If you are writing to another country, write the country in the address.

DATE: on the right. Various forms of the date are possible.

OPENING SALUTATION: Use the name of the reader if you know it, without the initial. If you do not, write *Dear Sirs* to a company, *Dear Sir* to a man, *Dear Madam* to a woman or *Dear Sir or Madam* if you do not know the sex of the reader.

BODY OF THE LETTER: Start a new paragraph for each new idea or subject. Leave a line space between each paragraph. Do not break words at the end of a line.

CLOSING SALUTATION: *Yours faithfully* if you do not know the reader's name, *Yours sincerely* if you do. (US *Yours truly* or *Sincerely yours.*)

SIGNATURE.

WRITER'S NAME AND TITLE (and position in the company, if appropriate). A man uses the title *Mr.* The title *Mrs* shows that a woman is married; *Miss* shows that she is unmarried; *Ms* shows only that she is a woman.

BLOCK STYLE is the modern style – all paragraphs start at the left-hand margin.

PUNCTUATION: in modern business letters punctuation is not used in the headings and endings of a letter. Normal punctuation is used in the body of the letter.

Unit Two
Buying and Selling

 Anne Bell is at Household Designs buying some crockery and cutlery for the office. She is talking to a sales assistant.

1 Can I help you?

Yes. I want to buy some crockery and cutlery for the office.

2 We have these plain dark blue ones.

They're too expensive, I'm afraid.

3 Do you give a discount?

Yes. I can give you 10%.

4 And can you deliver them?

Yes. We'll bring them round this afternoon.

5 Will you pay in cash or by cheque?

By cheque. I've got a cheque card.

6 Could you give me a receipt please?

Of course.

Exercise 2.1   *Listening comprehension*

Listen to the tape and choose the correct answer to each question:

1 Which word means cups, saucers and plates?
    (a) cutlery (b) crockery (c) furniture
2 How much did the small plain plates cost each?
    (a) £1.80 (b) £1.90 (c) 80p
3 Which crockery did Anne buy?
    (a) the flowered ones (b) the plain ones (c) the striped ones
4 How many items of crockery did Anne buy?
    (a) 10 (b) 20 (c) 60
5 How many items of cutlery did Anne buy?
    (a) 6 (b) 20 (c) 26
6 How did Anne pay?
    (a) in cash (b) by cheque (c) by cheque card

Exercise 2.2   *Receipts*

Listen to the tape again. Use the information from the tape and in the till receipt to decide which figures replace the small letters in the written receipt:

```
HOUSEHOLD
DESIGNS
        16.00
        16.00
        12.00
  S/T  44.00
  10%   4.40
  T    39.60
         3.00
         2.10
  T    44.70

  23/03/83
```

HOUSEHOLD
DESIGNS & CO LTD

22 High Street Manchester M1 2BL   001423

Date: 23 March 1983

Quantity	Description	Unit price £ p	Total price £ p
(a)	plates (ref. 67/BW)	(b)	(c)
(d)	cups (ref. 70/BW)	(e)	(f)
(g)	saucers (ref. 71/BW)	(h)	(i)
	Sub total		(j)
	Discount @ 10%		(k)
	Total		(l)
(m)	teaspoons (ref. 232)	(n)	(o)
(p)	Knives (ref. 235)	(q)	(r)
	Total		(s)
	Received with thanks G. Archer		

Exercise 2.3 *Sums of money*

Write these sums of money in full as you would say them or write them on a cheque, like this:

£23.60 *Twenty-three pounds sixty pence*
$18.20 *Eighteen dollars and twenty cents*

1	£79.30	4	$64.96	7	£85.41
2	£253	5	$2	8	£1,200
3	$569.50	6	£2,387	9	£790.90

NB When you write a whole number of pounds or dollars on a cheque, you write *only* afterwards to show that there are no pence or cents, eg *Six hundred pounds only.*

Laboratory drill
P: Number one   R: *Seventy-nine pounds, thirty pence*

Exercise 2.4 *Buying and selling*

Nick bought stereo equipment from Stereo Inc. The price of the speakers was $110 each. The bill for two speakers came to $220. He paid in cash. He gave the assistant $250 and she gave him $30 change and his receipt.

Write full sentences in answer to these questions, like this:

How much did each speaker cost? *Each speaker cost $110.*

1 What was the unit price of the speakers?
2 Who was the seller?
3 Who was the buyer?
4 Who was the customer?
5 How did Nick pay for the equipment?
6 How much did Nick spend?
7 How much did the bill come to?
8 How much change did the assistant give him?
9 What was Nick's purchase?
10 What did Nick purchase?
11 Who was the supplier?
12 What was Nick's proof of payment?

Exercise 2.5   A transaction

In pairs, ask and answer similar questions to the ones in Exercise 2.4 about Anne's transaction in Household Designs, like this:

P: *How much did each knife cost?*   R: *35 pence.*

Laboratory drill
P: Each knife cost 35 pence.   R: *How much did each knife cost?*

Exercise 2.6   Opposites

In pairs, talk about these adjectives and their opposites, like this:

P: *It's too short.*   R: *Oh I see. It's not long enough.*

1   expensive
2   big
3   wide
4   noisy
5   heavy

Laboratory drill A
P: It's too short.   R: *Oh I see. It's not long enough.*

Laboratory drill B
P: It's not long enough.   R: *Oh I see. It's too short.*

Exercise 2.7   Collective nouns; count and mass nouns

Which collective noun describes the examples on the left? The letters of the collective nouns are in the wrong order and the words are in the wrong place.

		Collective	
A	knives, forks, spoons	1	RUNEFRUIT
B	plates, cups, saucers	2	TYRCULE
C	pencils, paper, envelopes	3	YEOCCKRR
D	chairs, tables, desks	4	TARESTIONY
E	letters, memos, telexes	5	PIQUETMEN
F	calculators, photocopiers, typewriters	6	SOORRCCNNEEEPD

Choose the correct words to complete these sentences:

1   How *much/many* equipment have you got?
2   I would like twenty *knives/cutlery.*
3   Have you got *a/any* plain crockery?
4   There is *some/a* stationery over there.
5   I haven't got *much/many* paper.
6   There *was/were* only a few chairs.
7   There aren't many *desks/furniture.*
8   He didn't receive much *correspondence/letters.*

Exercise 2.8 *Cheques*

Anne Bell has an account at Bonds Bank. When she wants to pay money to someone, she writes a cheque. This is an order to the bank to pay money to someone from her account. You can write a cheque on anything (a man once wrote a cheque on a cow and the bank paid the money), but banks give standard cheque forms to customers who have accounts (account-holders).

Look at this cheque Anne paid into her account and give short answers to the questions:

Counts Bank plc   *28 March 1983*   90.10.109

Trafford Branch
89 Berry Road
Manchester M15 2PQ

Pay *Anne Bell*   or order

Four hundred and ninety-two pounds twenty- | £ 492-28 |

eight pence
_____ for and on behalf of
                                                    Transworld Freight plc

                                                    Liz Shepherd

Cheque no   Branch no   Account no
621517   90″10109   013378234

NB   Some of the questions mean the same. Which ones?

1   Who wrote the cheque?
2   When did she write the cheque?
3   Who is the payee?
4   Who does Liz Shepherd work for?
5   Whose account number is 013378234?
6   At which bank do Transworld have an account?
7   Who made out the cheque?
8   Who is the cheque made out to?
9   Who is the person receiving the money?
10   Who signed the cheque?
11   Who is the drawer?
12   Is 013378234 Liz Shepherd's account number?
13   Each branch of Counts has its own number. What is the number of the Trafford branch?
14   Whose signature is on the cheque?
15   What do you think the abbreviation *a/c* stands for? (The word is on the cheque.)

Exercise 2.9   *A simulation: Buying and selling*

Do this roleplay exercise in pairs. One student is Anne Bell and the other is a sales assistant. *If you are the sales assistant, turn immediately to the next page.*

Anne   You have received a memo from Graham Davis asking you to buy some furniture. Choose either of the memos below and *do not read the other one.* Take your information from the memo you have chosen and talk to the 'sales assistant' (do not show him the memo). You can choose from the chairs pictured below, but the sales assistant will tell you how much they cost and anything else you want to know. You must not pay more than the amount Graham says in the memo, but try and get the best terms you can.

INTERNAL MEMORANDUM
TO: Anne Bell
FROM: Graham Davis
DATE: 23 March 1983
SUBJECT: Office furniture

We need new chairs for visitors in the
reception area. Can you arrange it?
We need 10 comfortable chairs in either
blue or green. The maximum amount you
can spend is £600.

INTERNAL MEMORANDUM
TO: Anne Bell
FROM: Graham Davis
DATE: 23 March 1982
SUBJECT: Office furniture

We need some comfortable chairs for
visitors to go in the managers' offices.
Can you arrange it?
We need 10 chairs in either beige or
dark brown. The maximum you can spend is
£550.

Sales assistant (Mr Jones) Anne Bell wants to buy some chairs from you. This is the range you have in stock:

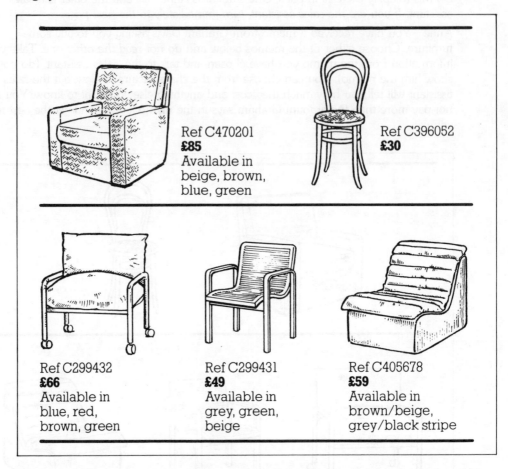

Ref C470201
£85
Available in
beige, brown,
blue, green

Ref C396052
£30

Ref C299432
£66
Available in
blue, red,
brown, green

Ref C299431
£49
Available in
grey, green,
beige

Ref C405678
£59
Available in
brown/beige,
grey/black stripe

You can offer a 10% discount on sales of £500 or over if you think it will help you get a sale. Do not show your catalogue to Anne. She has pictures of the chairs.

Start the conversation by saying to Anne: *Can I help you?*

When you have bought and sold the chairs you want, change roles (or change partners) and do the simulation again using the other memo.

Exercise 2.10   *More about cheques*

Today is 23 March. Anne wants to pay Household Designs £100, but she only has £50 in her account. She will have enough money in her account next week, so she writes a later date on the cheque (eg 31 March). This is called post-dating a cheque. It is now a post-dated cheque. The bank will not accept it before the date written.

Nick Dawson gave Anne Bell (the payee) a cheque for £10. Anne wanted to pay Tom Rowe £10. On the back of Nick's cheque she wrote, '*Pay Tom Rowe or order*' and then she signed her name. This is called endorsing a cheque. The cheque is endorsed to Tom Rowe. It is possible to endorse a cheque because of the words *or order* written on the front. This means the cheque is negotiable.

Some shops do not like taking cheques because the customer might be dishonest. Banks give most account-holders a guarantee card (also called a cheque card or a banker's card) which they sign. The shop assistant compares the signature on the cheque and on the card and writes the guarantee card number on the back of the cheque. The bank guarantees payment (up to £50) even if the account-holder does not have enough money in his/her account at the time.

Write a cheque to the person sitting on your right. Make up the name, branch and address of the bank and the computer numbers. When you receive the cheque from the person on your left, endorse it to someone else.

Exercise 2.11 *Word puzzle*

Use the clues to help you complete this word puzzle. Each number always represents the same letter, eg 1 = T, 2 = E.

```
[4 ]           [3 ][5 ][14][11][8 ][1 ][12][7 ][2 ]
[10]           [12]                    [11]    [6 ]
[3 ]     [9 ][7 ][8 ][16][2 ][7 ]              [9 ]    [20]
[1 ]     [11]         [7 ]                     [10][7 ][9 ][2 ][7 ]
[██]     [2 ]     [4 ][8 ][21][2 ][2 ]         [7 ]    [18]
[9 ]     [14]         [11]                     [3 ]    [12]
[8 ][6 ][6 ][10][12][11][1 ][██][20][10][15][9 ][2 ][7 ]    [2 ]
[1 ]     [1 ]         [2 ]
[2 ]     [5 ]         [2 ]                   [13]
[9 ][17][8 ][19][2 ][██][10][12][1 ]        [7 ]
         [13]        [6 ]                   [8 ]
         [15]        [8 ][6 ][6 ][10][12][11][1 ]
         [2 ]        [7 ]                   [6 ]
         [9 ]              [20]
```

Clues
A . . . . . . cheque has a later date on it
You sign a cheque with your . . . . . .
The payee writes the number of the . . . . . . on the back of the cheque so that the bank will definitely pay the money.
You . . . . . . a cheque when you sign your name on the back
An order to the bank to pay money to someone is a . . . . . .
The money comes out of the . . . . . .'s account when he/she writes a cheque
If a cheque is . . . . . . you can endorse it
The words 'or . . . . . .' mean you can endorse a cheque
The person the cheque is made out to is the . . . . . .
A person who has an account at a bank is an . . . . . .
One of the offices of a bank where you can pay in or draw out money is a . . . . . .
To write a cheque is to . . . . . . a cheque
A/c stands for . . . . . .

Unit 2

Exercise 2.12 *Mistakes*

Sandra Parr was away from work and Anne was busy, so a temporary typist typed this
letter. She made more than ten mistakes. Can you find them?

```
                                    Mr O Jones
                                    Household Designs & Co Ltd.
                                    22 High Street
                                    Manchester M1 2BL
                                    England


A. Bell
Transworld Freight plc
74 Dockside
Manchester                          24st march 1983


Our ref : AB/ts


Dear Sirs,

   Further to our meeting of yesterday, I would like to
place an order for 10 chairs (type C405678).  Can you su-
pply them in blue or green and can you offer a discount?

I look forward to hearing from you.

              Yours sincerely

              A. Bell

Enc
```

Language notes

Cardinal numbers

0	oh/zero/nought	10	ten	20	twenty
1	one	11	eleven	31	thirty-one
2	two	12	twelve	42	forty-two
3	three	13	thirteen	53	fifty-three
4	four	14	fourteen	164	a/one hundred and sixty-four
5	five	15	fifteen	475	four hundred and seventy-five
6	six	16	sixteen	986	nine hundred and eighty-six
7	seven	17	seventeen	697	six hundred ninety-seven (US)
8	eight	18	eighteen	100	a/one hundred
9	nine	19	nineteen	800	eight hundred

1,000 *a/one thousand*
10,000 *ten thousand*
100,000 *a/one hundred thousand*
1,000,000 *a/one million*
1,000,000,000 *a/one thousand million* (UK); *a/one billion* (US)
1,000,000,000,000 *a/one billion* (UK); *a/one trillion* (US)
276,984 *two hundred and seventy-six thousand, nine hundred and eighty-four*
Note the comma which separates each group of three numbers (starting from the right).

Sums of money

Notice the following points:
£62,573.22 $25.02   38p   67¢
The pound (£) or dollar ($) signs go before the numbers.
A decimal point (full stop) separates pounds from pence and dollars from cents.
We only write *p* or *¢* after sums of money when cents or pence are written alone without pounds or dollars, eg 6¢ (but $.06).

NB   *£3m = three million pounds*
$6.2m = six point two million dollars
or   *six million, two hundred thousand dollars*

Count and mass nouns (also called countable and uncountable nouns)

COUNT NOUNS
They have a singular and a plural:
A pencil/the pencil is on the table.
Please pass me the pencils.
There are five/some pencils on the table.

MASS NOUNS
They have only a singular or a plural, not both:
There is a lot of furniture.
There is some furniture in the room.
There are some scissors on the table.
The scissors are over there.

Note that you can talk about individual items which are mass nouns by using phrases such as *a piece of, an item of,* eg
There is a pair of *scissors on the table.*
A chair is an item of *furniture.*

NEGATIVE AND QUESTION

With count nouns: *Are there any pencils?*   *There are not any pencils.*
                     How many pencils are there?

With mass nouns: *Is there any furniture?*   *There is not any furniture.*
                     Are there any scissors?   *There are not any scissors.*
                     Are there any pieces of furniture?
                     Are there any pairs of scissors?
                     How much furniture is there?
                     How many pairs of scissors are there?

Irregular verbs first used in this unit

INFINITIVE (present)	PAST SIMPLE	PAST PARTICIPLE
buy	*bought*	*bought*
choose	*chose*	*chosen*
come	*came*	*come*
cost	*cost*	*cost*
draw	*drew*	*drawn*
read/ri:d/	*read*/rɛd/	*read*/rɛd/
show	*showed*	*shown*
stand	*stood*	*stood*

British English	**American English**
An *order* is a request for goods	A *purchase order* (po) is a request for goods
A *note* is a piece of paper money eg a £10 *note*. A *bill* is a request for payment	A *bill* is a piece of paper money eg a $10 *bill*
A *cheque* is an order to a bank to pay money to someone	A *check* is an order to a bank to pay money to someone. A *check* is also a bill received by a customer in a restaurant.
A *sales assistant* is someone who serves in a shop	A *sales clerk* is someone who serves in a shop

Unit Three
Transportation

 Nigel Storke is talking to Kevin Hughes at Transworld about transporting a consignment from Beeton to Norton.

1 Kevin Hughes speaking.

2 Good afternoon. My name's Nigel Storke from GLM Engineering.

Exercise 3.1 *Listening comprehension*

 Listen to the tape and decide which letter represents which town. Then mark the statements below true or false.

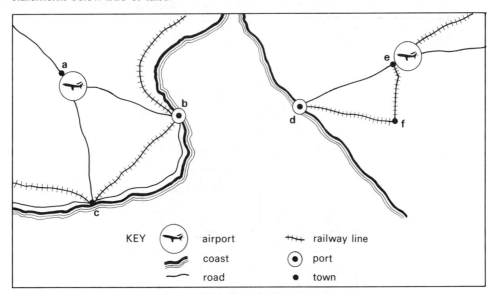

KEY — airport · railway line · coast · port · road · town

1 Beeton is on the coast.
2 Ayton is inland.
3 Easton is a port.
4 Weston is an airport.
5 There is an airport at Sutton.
6 There is a road between Beeton and Easton.
7 There is a port at Ayton
8 There is a railway line between Ayton and Norton.

Unit 3

Exercise 3.2 / *Transportation*

Kevin Hughes arranged for the transportation of a consignment of machinery by rail and sea. The place of departure was Beeton and the destination was Norton. The cargo (the freight) was 10 cases of machinery. The measurements of each case were 10 m by 2m by 1.1m, so the volume of the whole consignment was 220 cubic metres. Each case weighed 20 kilos, so the weight of the consignment was 200k. The freight rate was £1.50 per kilo or per cu metre, whichever was the greater. The charge by volume was £330 (220 m³ × £1.50) and the charge by weight was £300 (200k. × £1.50). However Kevin decided not to send the goods as conventional cargo because he could get a discount if he packed the goods in a standard sized container.

Use the clues to help you fill in this puzzle. All the words are in the text.

Clues

1 and 2 Two words meaning *cost*
3 The place the goods leave from is the place of . . . . . .
4 The place the goods are going to is the . . . . . .
5 A large box is also called a . . . . . .
6 To put goods into boxes ready for travelling is to . . . . . . them
7 The . . . . . . (size) of the consignment was 220 cu m
8 The . . . . . . of each case were 10 m × 2m × 1.1m
9 and 10 Goods packed separately, not in containers, are called . . . .
10 Goods travelling from one place to another are called a . . . . . .
11 This word has two meanings (a) goods travelling from one place to another (b) the cost of transporting goods from one place to another
12 How heavy something is
13 A large box of a standard size for transporting goods is called a . . . . . .
14 This word means usual, regular, always the same

Hidden word: Moving goods from one place to another

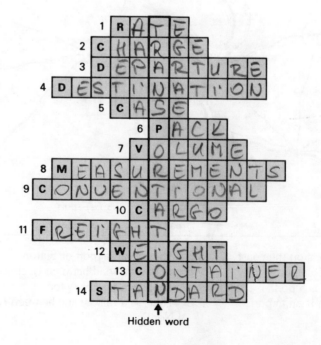

Hidden word

Exercise 3.3   *Questioning*

In pairs, ask and answer questions about the text in Exercise 3.2, like this:
Ask about the consignment.

P: *What was the consignment?*   R: *Machinery*

Ask about   1 the number of cases   6 the weight of each case
            2 the means of transport   7 the freight rate
            3 the measurements of the cases   8 the weight of the consignment
            4 the volume of each case   9 the charge by volume
            5 the volume of the consignment   10 the charge by weight

---

Laboratory drill
P: Ask about the consignment.   R: *What was the consignment?*

Exercise 3.4   *Problem-solving*

Work out the answers to these questions. Take any information you need from the text in Exercise 3.2.

1   The charge by volume is £33. The charge by weight is £300. Which rate will Kevin pay?   £ 300

2   When he sent the goods in a container, Kevin got a 10% discount on the conventional cargo price. How much did he pay?   £ 270

3   Containers come in two main sizes (a) a 20-foot (6-metre) container is 2.4 × 2.4 × 5.9m (b) a 40-foot (12-metre) container is 2.4 × 2.4 × 12m. Which size container did Kevin use? Draw the container and draw how you think the cases were packed in it.

4   I want to send some goods which weigh 100k and which measure 30 m³. The cost is 50p per kilo or per cubic metre. How much will the freight be?   £ 50

5   I want to send a cargo which weighs 5 tonnes and which measures 10 m³. The charge is $1 per tonne or 50¢ per cubic metre. How much will it cost?   5 pounds

6   Do you think these goods are usually charged by weight or by volume?
    (a) fruit   (b) potatoes   (c) bags of sand   (d) shoes

7   The freight rate from Beeton to Norton for one consignment is £1.50 per kilo or per cubic metre. The freight rate from Easton to Ayton for another consignment is £2. What reasons can you think of for the different freight rates?   distance, the way of transportation

8   Can you think of any advantages or disadvantages for sending goods in containers or as conventional cargo?   if the consignment is very small

Exercise 3.5   *Dimensions*

Write these dimensions (measurements) in full as you say them and give the area or volume, like this:

23 × 12m   *Twenty-three by twelve. That's two hundred and seventy-six square metres.*
9.5 × 2 × 5cm   *Nine point five by two by five. That's ninety-five cubic centimetres.*

1   16 × 5cm   5   1.1 × 5k
2   30 × 2.5 × 1m   6   60 × 12 × 10cm
3   20 × 4 × 30cm   7   7 × 1 × 1k
4   19 × 0.1m   8   20 × 2k

Laboratory drill
P: Number one   R: *Sixteen by five centimetres*

Exercise 3.6   *Used to do*

In pairs, talk about things in the past which are not true now, like this:

P: *There isn't an airport at Ayton nowadays.*
R: *Did there use to be an airport at Ayton then?*
P: *There used to be, but there isn't any more.*

P: *She has only worked for GLM since the takeover.*
R: *Didn't she use to work for GLM then?*
P: *She didn't use to, but she does now.*

1 They don't handle dangerous cargo since the accident.
2 Transworld send containerised goods nowadays.
3 There isn't a railway line between Dutton and Norton any more.
4 He doesn't export to Italy now.
5 Transworld arrange airfreight consignments these days.
6 They make stereo equipment since they expanded.

> *Laboratory drill*
> P: There isn't an airport at Ayton nowadays.   R: *Did there use to be an airport at Ayton then?*

Exercise 3.7   *Comparing*

This table shows the comparative speed and cost of sending a consignment of cloth from London to Madrid.

MEANS OF TRANSPORT	TRANSIT TIME	FREQUENCY OF DEPARTURE	TOTAL COST
	10 days	Every 12 days	£246
	1 day	Every day	£433
	4 days	Every 5 days	£149
	3 days	Every 7 days	£145

In pairs, compare the different means of sending the consignment, like this:

P: *Is it quicker by sea than by air?*   R: *No. It's slower.*
P: *Are trains more frequent than trailers?*   R: *No. They're less frequent.*
P: *Is it more expensive by train than by*
   plane?   R: *No. It's less expensive.*

> *Laboratory drill*
> P: Is it quicker by sea than by air?   R: *No. It's slower.*

Exercise 3.8   *Sending a consignment*

You are sending the consignment in Exercise 3.7. Decide which method of transport you will choose. Say why you think this method is the best and why you did not choose the other methods.

Exercise 3.9 *Reported speech and used to do*

In pairs, discuss John's out-of-date knowledge, like this:

There's an airport at Dutton.

P: John said there was an airport at Dutton.
R: He's wrong then. There used to be an airport at Dutton, but there isn't now.

She doesn't work for BOS.

P: John said she didn't work for BOS.
R: He's wrong then. She didn't use to work for BOS, but she does now.

1 *They handle dangerous cargo.*

2 *Transworld don't send containerised goods.*

3 *There's a railway line between Dutton and Freetown.*

4 *He exports to Spain.*

5 *Transworld don't arrange airfreight consignments.*

6 *They don't make computers.*

Laboratory drill A
P: John said there was an airport at Dutton.
R: *There used to be an airport at Dutton, but there isn't now.*
P: John said she didn't work for BOS.
R: *She didn't use to work for BOS, but she does now.*

Laboratory drill B
P: I think there's an airport at Dutton.   R: *Yes. John said there was an airport at Dutton.*

P: I don't think she works for BOS.   R: *Yes. John said she didn't work for BOS.*

Unit 3

Exercise 3.10   *Containerisation*

Decide which of these words and phrases goes in which gap in this text about containerisation:

1   2   3   4   5   6   7
so – but – for example – This is because – As a result – On the other hand – Also –
8   9
because – also

Many big ports today are containerised, [1] *for example* ......, in Britain Tilbury (London) and Southampton can handle containers. The handling of containers has many advantages over conventional cargo.

It takes fewer men to handle containers than to load and unload conventional cargoes [2] *so* ... it is quicker. A hundred men take about three weeks to unload and load a conventional ship, [3] *but* ...... it only takes fifteen men about four days to unload and load a container ship. [4] *This is because* ...... there is special loading equipment. There are special container carriers in all kinds of transport: road-trailers, special railway waggons, and container ships. There are [5] *also* ...... containers specially designed to fit in aeroplanes. At his place of business the exporter packs the goods into a container which is not opened until it arrives at its destination. [6] *As a result* ...... fewer goods are stolen and fewer goods are damaged when they are sent in containers.

Wage bills are lower [7] *because* ...... you need fewer men to handle the goods. [8] *On the other hand* ...... more people are out-of-work. There is more unemployment. [9] *Also* ...... the special equipment for handling containers is very expensive and most ports are still not specially adapted for container traffic.

Write a summary (a shorter version) of this text. Leave out all the examples and all repetition of ideas (the same thing said in a different way). Make sure you keep all the important information.

Exercise 3.11   *Note-taking*

Draw a table like this and write in the advantages and disadvantages of containerisation and conventional cargo in note form.

	CONVENTIONAL CARGO	CONTAINERISED TRANSPORT
ADVANTAGES		quicker *cheaper safer*
DISADVANTAGES	slower	more unemployment

Discuss the advantages and disadvantages, like this:

On the one hand containerised transport is quicker, but on the other hand there is more unemployment.

and like this:

Although containerised transport is quicker, there is more unemployment.

Exercise 3.12   *Oral (and written) presentation*

Listen to the talk on the tape about the disadvantages of containerised transport. Prepare yourself to give a similar short talk (one or two minutes) about any of these subjects:

1 The advantages of conventional cargo
2 The disadvantages of conventional cargo
3 The advantages of containerised transport

Take turns to name any other student and say which of the three subjects he/she must talk about. Students may use their notes from Exercise 3.11, but they must not write out their talk beforehand. It is all right to give examples and repeat information in a different way in a talk.

Write a paragraph about one of the subjects.

Language notes

Comparatives and superlatives

		COMPARATIVE	SUPERLATIVE
SHORT WORDS	*small*	*smaller*	*the smallest*
	wide	*wider*	*the widest*
	heavy	*heavier*	*the heaviest*
	big	*bigger*	*the biggest*
LONG WORDS	*expensive*	*more expensive*	*the most expensive*
		less expensive	*the least expensive*
IRREGULAR	*good*	*better*	*the best*
	bad	*worse*	*the worst*
	some	*more*	*the most*
	a little (with mass nouns)	*less*	*the least*
	a few (with count nouns)	*fewer*	*the fewest*

Used to do

Used to + infinitive expresses something which happened or was true for some time in the past, but which is not true or happening now.

She used to work for BOS, but she does not work for them now.

QUESTION
Did she use to work for BOS?
or *Did she used to work for BOS?*

NEGATIVE
She did not use to work for BOS.
or *She did not used to work for BOS.*

Reported speech (also called indirect speech)

VERB OF SAYING	SPOKEN WORDS (DIRECT SPEECH)	REPORTED (INDIRECT) SPEECH
PRESENT SIMPLE *He says,*	+ ALL TENSES 'She likes coffee.' 'She was there.' 'They're going to leave.'	NO TENSE CHANGE He says she likes coffee. He says she was there. He says they're going to leave.
PAST SIMPLE *John said,* *Mary said,*	+ PRESENT SIMPLE 'She likes tea.' + TENSES WITH 'TO BE' 'He is working.' 'They are going to leave.' + PAST SIMPLE/PRESENT PERFECT 'He has met them.' 'He saw her.'	PAST SIMPLE John said she liked tea. PAST TENSE OF 'TO BE' Mary said he was working. Mary said they were going to leave. PAST PERFECT Mary said he had met them. Mary said he had seen her.

NB
1 *He said, 'I like tea.' → He said he liked tea.*
2 In reported speech you can also use *that* before the spoken words, eg *He said that he liked tea.*
3 The tense changes for reported speech are the same after verbs such as *think* and *know*, eg *I knew you were there. They thought she was going to leave.*

Irregular verbs first introduced in this unit

INFINITIVE	PAST SIMPLE	PAST PARTICIPLE
go	*went*	*gone/been*
keep	*kept*	*kept*
leave	*left*	*left*
think	*thought*	*thought*

British English	**American English**
The full form of *plane* is *aeroplane*	The full form of *plane* is *airplane*
Trains run on a *railway line* and goods are transported in *railway waggons*	Trains run on a *railroad track* and goods are transported in *railroad cars*
A *lorry* or *trailer* is a large vehicle for carrying goods by road	A *truck* is a large vehicle for carrying goods by road

Unit Four
Insurance

 Kathy Joyce is interviewing David Constable on a television programme called 'Introduction to Business'.

On today's programme we have David Constable, who is going to talk about insurance.

The history of insurance in Britain is a long one.

Then there was the Great Fire of London.

Today Lloyd's is the name of a famous insurance market in London.

Customers and underwriters used to arrange insurance in a coffee house which belonged to a man called Lloyd.

In the early days there was a lot of marine trade between Britain and India and America.

Unit 4

Exercise 4.1   *Listening comprehension*

Listen to the tape and put pictures 3 to 6 on page 29 in the right order.
Which date goes with which picture?
(a) the 16th century   (b) the 17th century   (c) the 18th century
(d) the 20th century
Mark these statements true or false.
1   The first kind of insurance was fire insurance.
2   Insuring ships is called marine insurance.
3   The first fire brigades were employed by insurance companies.
4   The people who arrange insurance are called brokers.
5   The people who actually insure property are called brokers.
6   Lloyd's is a coffee house.

Exercise 4.2   *Roman numerals*

What numbers do these roman numerals stand for? Put them in two columns of odd
and even numbers in numerical order, starting with the lowest number in each column.

(a) III   (b) XX   (c) VI   (d) IX   (e) XVII   (f) XIV
(g) IV   (h) XIX   (i) XII   (j) XI   (k) II   (l) X

ODD NUMBERS   EVEN NUMBERS
(a) *III – 3*   (k) *II – 2*

NB   Even numbers are numbers which can be divided exactly by two.

> *Laboratory drill*
> P: Fourteen   R: *XIV*

Exercise 4.3   *Years and centuries*

In pairs, talk about these years and centuries, like this:

P: *Sixteen sixty-six*   R: *That's in the seventeenth century.*

(a) 1666   (b) 1952   (c) 2000   (d) 1874   (e) 1739   (f) 1225   (g) 1983   (h) 25 BC

> *Laboratory drill A*
> P: Sixteen sixty-six   R: *That's in the seventeenth century.*
>
> *Laboratory drill B*
> P: (a)   R: *Sixteen sixty-six*

Exercise 4.4   *Dates*

Write these dates as you would say them if you were (a) British (b) American, like this:

6/12   (a) *The sixth of December*   (b) *June twelfth*
(i) 8/9   (ii) 3/7   (iii) 10/2   (iv) 11/1   (v) 4/12   (vi) 5/5

> *Laboratory drill A*
> P: Six stroke twelve   R: *The sixth of December*
>
> *Laboratory drill B*
> P: Six stroke twelve   R: *June twelfth*

Exercise 4.5   *Insurance*

Mr Bean wanted to insure his shop. He wanted ¹...... cover against fire and theft. He
filled in the ²...... form and sent it to his ³...... broker who arranged the insurance with
an ⁴....... Mr Bean had to pay quite a high ⁵...... premium each year, but it was worth
it because a lot of goods were stolen. Mr Bean put in a ⁶...... for ⁷...... compensation
Unfortunately, the ⁸....... refused to pay him the full amount. Mr Bean had not
read the ⁹...... in his ¹⁰...... properly.

Find out (use a dictionary) which definition on the right matches which word on the left.
Decide which word goes in which gap in the passage above.

a	premium	i	A person who advises on insurance
b	underwriter	ii	A document which proves you are insured
c	insurance company	iii	Payment for insurance
d	broker	iv	Insurance protection
e	claim	v	A form you fill in when you apply for insurance
f	compensation	vi	An insurer at Lloyd's of London
g	small print	vii	A limited liability company selling cover
h	policy/insurance	viii	The conditions and clauses in a document
	certificate		of insurance, usually in small writing
i	proposal form	ix	You are paid ...... when your insured property
			is damaged
j	cover	x	A request for payment when your insured
			property is damaged

Exercise 4.6   *Phrasal verbs*

Decide which phrasal verb replaces the more formal verbs in italics in these sentences. In
pairs, use the phrasal verbs with nouns and with pronouns, like this:

To *effect* insurance cover

P: *I'm going to take out insurance cover.*   R: *Let me take it out for you.*

take out – fill in – turn off – put in – work out – take off – look up

1   To *submit* a claim
2   To *deduct* the discount
3   To *complete* the form
4   To *calculate* the premium
5   To *find* the word
6   To *stop* the photocopier

Laboratory drill
P: I'm going to take out insurance cover.   R: *Let me take it out for you.*

Unit 4

Exercise 4.7 *Correspondence*

The following correspondence is all related to one insurance transaction. Decide in which order the items were sent and where the following dates and phrases go:

a 10 August
b 11 August
c 11 August 1983
d 15 August
e 15 August 1983
f 17.8.83
g 18 August

h 18 August 1983
i 22 August 1983
j 29 August
k 6.9.83
l 7 September 1983

m to receiving your premium.
n to hearing from you.
o to receiving the insurance certificate.
p to doing business with you in the future.

NB Do not worry about words you do not know as long as you understand the message.

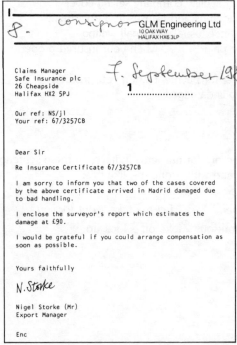

I

consignor **GLM Engineering Ltd**
10 OAK WAY
HALIFAX HX6 3LP

Claims Manager
Safe Insurance plc
26 Cheapside
Halifax HX2 5PJ

7. September 1983

1 ....

Our ref: NS/jl
Your ref: 67/3257CB

Dear Sir

Re Insurance Certificate 67/3257CB

I am sorry to inform you that two of the cases covered by the above certificate arrived in Madrid damaged due to bad handling.

I enclose the surveyor's report which estimates the damage at £90.

I would be grateful if you could arrange compensation as soon as possible.

Yours faithfully

N. Storke

Nigel Storke (Mr)
Export Manager

Enc

II

SAFE INSURANCE PLC
26 CHEAPSIDE
HALIFAX HX2 5PJ

Mr N Storke
Export Manager
GLM Engineering Ltd
10 Oak Way
Halifax HX6 3LP

2 15 august 1983 ....

Our ref: 67/3257CB
Your ref: NS/jl

Dear Mr Storke

Thank you for your letter of **3** 11 of August ....

I am pleased to inform you that we will insure your shipment to Madrid as requested. The premium for all risk cover from warehouse to warehouse is at the rate of 2% of the sum assured.

I look forward **4** to receiving your premium ....

Yours sincerely

GCook

Geoffrey Cook (Mr)
Premiums Manager

III

TELEPHONE MESSAGES

TO: Nigel agent consignee
FROM: Carlos Perez, Madrid Imports
TELEPHONE NUMBER: ‒
MESSAGE: Please arrange insurance for the cargo to Madrid
DATE: **5** 10 of August ....
TAKEN BY: Jenny

IV 7.

6.9.83

```
GLM ENGING 22819G
MADRID IMP 62502S MADRID  6........ 1420
ATTN STORKE
TWO CASES DAMAGED IN TRANSIT DUE TO BAD HANDLING.
ESTIMATED DAMAGE EIGHTY POUNDS. PLS CLAIM ON
INSURANCE. SURVEYORS REPORT FOLLWS +
REGARDS
PEREZ
MADRID IMP 62502S
GLM ENGING 22819G
```

V 4.

17.8.83

```
MADRID IMP 62502S
GLM ENGING 22819G HALIFAX  7......... 1035
ATTN PEREZ
INSURANCE ARRANGED AT TWO PERCENT CHARGED TO YOU +
REGARDS
STORKE
GLM ENGING 22819G
MADRID IMP 62502S
```

VI 2

GLM Engineering Ltd
10 OAK WAY
HALIFAX HX6 3LP

Safe Insurance plc
26 Cheapside
Halifax HX2 5PJ

8 11 August 1983

Our ref: NS/jl
Your ref:

Dear Sirs

We are sending a consignment of 10 cases of machinery from Manchester to Madrid by rail on 9 29 of August

I would be grateful if you could arrange insurance cover for the goods at your best terms against all risks in transit for their value of £800. — lowest prices

I look forward 10 to hearing from you

Yours faithfully

N Storke

N Storke (Mr)
Export Manager

VII 6.

SAFE INSURANCE PLC
26 CHEAPSIDE
HALIFAX HX2 5PJ

Mr N Storke
Export Manager
GLM Engineering Ltd
10 Oak Way
Halifax HX6 3LP

22 August 1983

11
....

Our ref: 67/3257CB
Your ref: NC/jl

Dear Mr Storke

Re Insurance Certificate 67/3257CB

Thank you for your letter of 12 18 August .... and for the cheque for £16 in payment of the premium. I enclose the above certificate.

I look forward 13 to doing business with you in the future

Yours sincerely

G Cook

Geoffrey Cook (Mr)
Premiums Manager

Enc

VIII 5.

GLM Engineering Ltd
10 OAK WAY
HALIFAX HX6 3LP

Mr G Cook
Premiums Manager
Safe Insurance plc
26 Cheapside
Halifax HX2 5PJ

18 August 1983

14
....

Our ref: NS/jl
Your ref: 67/3257CB

Dear Mr Cook

Thank you for your letter of 15 15 August ....

I enclose a cheque for £16 in payment of the premium for insuring our consignment of machinery to Madrid.

I look forward 16 to receiving the insurance certificate

Yours sincerely

N Storke

Nigel Storke (Mr)
Export Manager

Enc

Exercise 4.8 *Summarising correspondence*

Use this table to help you summarise the correspondence in Exercise 4.7 as if you were giving a message to a colleague, like this:

i) *Mr Storke has written asking you to arrange compensation for two damaged cases.*

Mr Storke	ring	enclose	Please arrange compensation for two damaged cases.
			Please claim for two damaged cases.
Mr Cook	write	say	I will insure your shipment at 2%.
			Here is your insurance certificate.
Mr Perez	telex	ask	Please arrange insurance for a consignment to Madrid.
			Here is a cheque for the premium.
			I have arranged insurance at 2%.

Exercise 4.9 *Parts of a telex*

Give examples of these parts of a telex from telex (iv) in Exercise 4.7, like this:

Sender's answer back code (writer's address): *GLM ENGING 22819 G*

The equivalent part of a business letter is in brackets.

1 Receiver's answer back code (reader's address)
2 Date and time (date)
3 Opening salutation (*Dear* . . .)
4 Message (body of the letter)
5 Closing salutation (*Yours sincerely*)

NB You type your own answer back code and wait for your receiver's answer back code again at the end of the telex.

Exercise 4.10 *Giving information in letters*

Rewrite this information using standard business phrases according to whether the information is good or bad for the reader, like this:

We will arrange insurance for you.
I am pleased to inform you that we will arrange insurance for you.
We cannot arrange insurance for you.
I am sorry to inform you that we cannot arrange insurance for you.

1 The consignment was damaged.
2 We will pay the compensation in full.
3 Your insurance policy is out of date.
4 The goods were stolen.
5 The ship arrived late.
6 We are placing an order with you.

Exercise 4.11   *A simulation: Broking and underwriting*

Half the class are insurance brokers and half are underwriters at Lloyd's.

Brokers   Decide from this table which goods you are sending on which ship:

SHIP	FROM–TO	CARGO	VALUE
Tokyo Queen	Tokyo–Rio de Janeiro	Computer parts	
~~SS Sydney Harbour~~	~~London–Sydney~~	~~Stereo equipment~~	
Canada Bay	Hamburg–Ottawa	Cassette recorders	£5,000
New York Express	New York–Alexandria	Car parts	
La Genovese	Genoa–Buenos Aires	Motorbikes	

Write the details at the top of a broker's slip like the one below. You will go to the underwriters at Lloyd's and try to get the best premium for insuring your cargo. Give the underwriters who insure you an IOU for the premium you will pay them (see below).

Underwriters   You can only insure amounts of £2,500 at a time, but you can choose your premium rate: £2,500 @ 1.5% = £37.50
@ 2%   = £50
@ 2.5% = £62.50

You want to collect the highest premium you can, but if you charge too much brokers will not insure with you. You may not insure cargo worth more than £10,000 in total.

Everyone   Discuss with your teacher what sort of things brokers and underwriters will say. The market is only open for ten minutes, so you must not take too long arranging the insurance. The completed broker's slips should look like the one below. The winners are the underwriters who collect the highest premiums and the brokers who pay the least. Remember – it is possible that one of the ships will sink. In this case, the Lutine Bell (a ship's bell at Lloyd's) will ring and the name of the lost ship will be announced. Brokers whose ship sinks cannot win because their customers will not be able to deliver goods on time. Underwriters who insure goods on a ship which sinks cannot win because they must pay compensation.

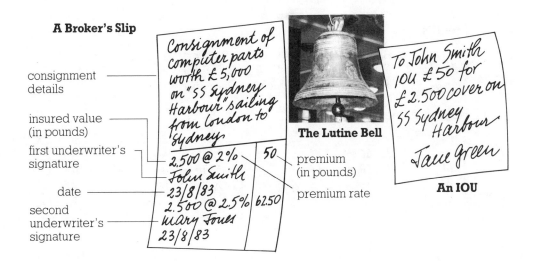

A Broker's Slip

consignment details ———

Consignment of computer parts worth £5,000 on "SS Sydney Harbour" sailing from London to Sydney

insured value (in pounds) ———

first underwriter's signature ———

*2,500 @ 2%   50
John Smith*

date ———

23/8/83

second underwriter's signature ———

*2,500 @ 2.5% 62.50
Mary Jones
23/8/83*

The Lutine Bell

premium (in pounds)

premium rate

*To John Smith IOU £50 for £2,500 cover on SS Sydney Harbour
Jane green*

An IOU

35

Unit 4

Exercise 4.12   *Vocabulary puzzle*

The clues for this word puzzle are on the tape. All the words are in this unit.

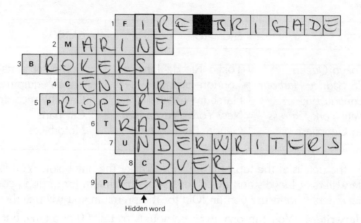

Hidden word

Language notes

Ordinal numbers

1st	first	7th	seventh	13th	thirteenth
2nd	second	8th	eighth	20th	twentieth
3rd	third	9th	ninth	31st	thirty-first
4th	fourth	10th	tenth	42nd	forty-second
5th	fifth	11th	eleventh	53rd	fifty-third
6th	sixth	12th	twelfth	64th	sixty-fourth

Other ordinal numbers are made by adding *th* to the cardinal number unless they end in 1, 2 or 3 (*first, second* or *third*).

Months

January	April	July	October
February	May	August	November
March	June	September	December

Roman numerals

1	I	6	VI	11	XI	16	XVI	30	XXX	84	LXXXIV
2	II	7	VII	12	XII	17	XVII	40	XL	90	XC
3	III	8	VIII	13	XIII	18	XVIII	49	XLIX	100	C
4	IV	9	IX	14	XIV	19	XIX	50	L	500	D
5	V	10	X	15	XV	20	XX	62	LXII	1,000	M

Present perfect tense

We use the present perfect for a past action which has an effect on the present. What happened and its effect on the present is more important than the time it happened (when the time in the past is important we use the past simple). The present perfect is made with the present tense of the verb *have* + past participle.

POSITIVE   *She has already typed the report. I know about Rome because I've been there.*
QUESTION   *Have you done it yet? Where have you been?*
NEGATIVE   *They have not come yet. He has never been there.*
SHORT ANSWER   *Yes I have. No he hasn't.*

Irregular verbs first introduced in this unit

INFINITIVE	PAST SIMPLE	PAST PARTICIPLE
find	*found*	*found*
sink	*sank*	*sunk*
steal	*stole*	*stolen*
understand	*understood*	*understood*

British English	American English
Note the spelling of *although*, *though* and *through* and such words as *kilometre* and *centre* Note the spelling of television *programme*, but computer *program*	Note the spelling of *altho*, *tho* and *thru* and such words as *kilometer* and *center* *Program* always has the same spelling

Unit Five
Sales Documentation

 At Transworld, Sandra Parr is taking a call from Liz Shepherd on the internal line.

1. Sandra here.

2. Oh hello, Sandra. It's Liz. Could I speak to Anne please?

3. I'm afraid she's not here at the moment. Can I take a message?

4. No. I'll ring her back later... No I won't.

5. Yes. Will you give her a message please?

6. Oh wait a minute, Liz. She's just come in.

Exercise 5.1   *Immediate reported speech*

Listen to the tape and complete the things Sandra says:

Liz says she [1]...... an invoice for some furniture, but she [2]...... the order.
Anne says she [3]...... a letter of order. She [4]...... an order form. She [5]...... an order number, but Liz says she [6]...... it.
Anne says she also [7]...... some cutlery and she [8]...... an official order, but she [9]...... by cheque and she [10]...... a receipt.
Liz says she's got the receipt and that's all right.

NB   The last sentence is in the past tense on the tape.

Exercise 5.2   *Reported speech in the past*

When Sandra gave Graham Davis a memo from Liz about sending order forms to the accounts department, he asked her what it was about. She told him about the morning's telephone conversations. Rewrite the things Liz and Anne said in Exercise 5.1, like this:

Liz said she'd got an order for some furniture, but . . .

Laboratory drill
P: *Liz says she's got an order for some furniture.*
R: *Liz said she'd got an order for some furniture.*

Exercise 5.3   *Telephoning*

Draw a table like this and fill in the words you think people actually say. Make up a name and telephone number for the caller. Some of the phrases in the introductory cartoon might be useful.

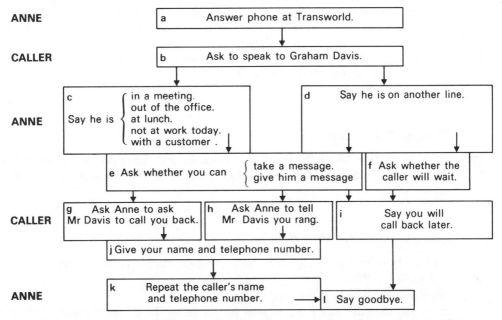

In pairs, practise making telephone calls when the person the caller wants to speak to is not available. Make up suitable names and telephone numbers.

Exercise 5.4 *Sales documentation*

When you travel by train, you need a ticket as proof that you have paid. When you send a consignment of goods by rail or road you also need a receipt to prove the transport company has taken the goods. A *consignment note* is both a ticket and a receipt. A consignment note for goods sent by air is called an *air consignment note* or an *air waybill*. A consignment note for goods sent by sea is a *Bill of Lading*. A *combined transport document* is for goods sent by more than one means of transport.

When companies buy goods, they send an *order* to the suppliers. If the buyers are regular customers, the suppliers send the goods and then send an *invoice*. The buyers do not always pay the invoice immediately. Usually the suppliers send a *statement* at the end of the month which shows all the transactions between the suppliers and the buyers in that month. The buyers then pay the amount outstanding on the statement.

Sometimes when the suppliers receive an enquiry, they send a *pro-forma invoice*. This is a quotatation which looks like the final invoice so the buyers know how much they have to pay. If the suppliers do not know the buyers, the buyers might pay in advance against the pro-forma when placing their order.

These questions refer to the words in italics in the text:

1 Which ones are requests for payment?
2 Which ones are a sort of ticket for transporting goods?
3 Which two mean exactly the same thing?
4 Which one is a request for goods?
5 Which ones are receipts for goods?
6 Transworld in Manchester is a regular customer of BOS in London. BOS usually sends goods by train. Which documents will be used when they do business?
7 Household Designs in Manchester sent goods to a customer in Liverpool by trailer. This was the first time the customer had bought anything from Household Designs. Which documents do you think were used?
8 Household Designs sent goods by air to a regular customer in France. Which documents do you think were used?

Exercise 5.5 *You*

 Listen to the tape. When the speakers say *you*, do they mean (a) the listener or (b) anyone in this situation? After each BLEEP write the sentence number and (a) or (b).

Exercise 5.6 *Relative clauses*

Decide which sentence on the right refers to which word in italics and rewrite the sentences, like this:

Anne sent *an order* to Household Designs.
Anne sent an order, which is a request for goods, to Household Designs.
Jane made out *an air waybill*.
Jane made out an air waybill, which is the ticket and receipt for goods sent by air.

1 GLM paid *the pro-forma invoice* before they received the goods.	It is a receipt for goods in transit.
	It is a request for goods.
2 Transworld received *a statement.*	It is the consignment note for goods sent by sea.
3 Anne gave *the invoice* to Liz in the accounts department.	It is used for goods sent by more than one means of transport.
4 Kevin asked for *the Bill of Lading.*	It showed all their transactions.
5 BOS usually send goods by rail with a *consignment note.*	It is a request for payment.
6 Jane made out the *combined transport document.*	It is the ticket and receipt for goods sent by air.
	It showed what the goods cost.

Exercise 5.7 *Past perfect tense*

Anne passed her exams and then she left school. After that she went to secretarial college and then she worked in a bank. Later she lived in London and finally she moved to Manchester and got a job with Transworld.

In pairs, discuss Anne's life, like this:

P: *Had Anne left school before she passed her exams?*
R: *No. She'd passed her exams before she left school.*
or *No. She left school after she'd passed her exams.*

Laboratory drill
P: Had Anne left school before she passed her exams?
R: *No. She'd passed her exams before she left school.*

P: Did Anne pass her exams after she'd left school?
R: *No. She left school after she'd passed her exams.*

Exercise 5.8 *More about the past perfect*

Decide which of these events happened before the other and combine the sentences using the past perfect, like this:

GLM sent the invoice. GLM sent the goods.
GLM sent the invoice after they had sent the goods.

1 BOS received the order. BOS sent the goods.
2 BOS sent the statement. Transworld received the goods.
3 Anne received the goods. Anne paid the pro-forma invoice.
4 Mr Perez received the goods by air. Mr Perez sent an order.
5 Transworld received the statement. Transworld paid BOS.
6 Kevin received the order. Kevin made out the Bill of Lading.

Laboratory drill
P: GLM sent the invoice. GLM sent the goods.
R: *GLM sent the invoice after they'd sent the goods.*

Unit 5

Exercise 5.9 *An invoice*

INVOICE

Invoice no: 0455/0004
Order no: 009762
Date: 05/04/83

HOUSEHOLD DESIGNS & CO LTD

22 High St Manchester M1 2BL

Tel: (061) 763 2555 Telex: 668542 HODES
Cables/telegrams: HODES MANCHESTER

TO: Transworld Freight plc
    74 Dockside
    Manchester M15 7BJ

Qty	Description	Unit price	Amount
5	chairs ref C299432B (blue)	£66	£330
5	chairs ref C299432G (green)	£66	£330
10% discount for payment received within one calendar month	Please quote invoice number when submitting payment	TOTAL	£660

The words in this puzzle are the full form of the abbreviations and symbols in the invoice, eg *no* in the invoice is *number* in the puzzle. Each number in the puzzle always stands for the same letter, eg 8 = E. What do the other numbers stand for and what are the words?

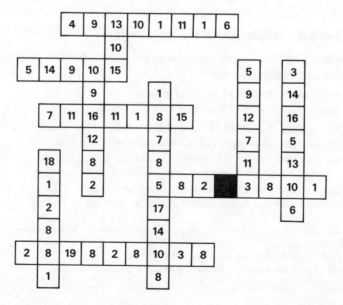

Exercise 5.10   *Comprehension*

Give short answers to these questions about the invoice in Exercise 5.9.
1   What is the name of the supplier?
2   What is the name of the buyer?
3   What date was the invoice sent?
4   How many chairs did Transworld buy?
5   How much did one chair cost?
6   If Transworld paid the invoice on 10 May 1983, how much did they pay?
7   If Transworld paid the invoice on 20 April 1983, how much did they pay?
8   When Transworld paid, what number did they send with the payment?

Exercise 5.11   *An order*

An order looks very similar to an invoice. Decide which information on the invoice in Exercise 5.9 also appeared on the order. Draw the order you think Transworld sent.

Exercise 5.12   *A memorandum*

This memorandum was accidentally put through the shredder. Rearrange the pieces and rewrite the memo with the correct layout (look at the memos in Exercise 2.9 if necessary). Five small pieces of the memo are missing. Can you work out what they are?

> Thank
>
> would be grateful if all staff could remember
>
> the accounts department.
>
> MEMORANDUM
>
> We need the order, which is our proof that someone
>
> for the office.
>
> the invoice. Please send a copy of each order to
>
> DATE: 11
>
> TO: All staff
>
> to use an official order form when they buy goods
>
> SUBJECT: *Liz Shepherd*
>
> in the office ordered the goods, before we can pay
>
> FROM: Liz Shepherd, Senior

Language notes

Past perfect tense

We use the past perfect about something which happened in the past before a certain time or before something else happened. The past perfect is made from *had* + past participle.

POSITIVE   *I had talked to him before we met.*
QUESTION   *Had you met him before 1973?*
NEGATIVE   *They had not seen him before that time.*
SHORT ANSWER   *Yes he had. No I hadn't.*

Non-defining relative clauses

A non-defining relative clause contains additional information about something or someone in a sentence. We use the relative pronoun *which* to start a relative clause about a thing and *who* about a person. There is a comma before the relative pronoun.

She sent the order. (An order is a request for goods.)
She sent the order, which is a request for goods.
She saw the accountant. (The accountant was very tall.)
She saw the accountant, who was very tall.

Consolidation A

Transworld News

TRANSWORLD NEWS

Why aren't you answering the phone?

There's no point. It's always for you.

What is different about the roman numerals on a clock face?

This advertisement appeared in a national paper recently. Can you find the ten typing errors they made?

Our frieght forarding bussiness is expanding and we need a AIRFREIHT CLARK. If you have experiense in this tipe of work, contact Graham Davis, Asistant Maneger, Transworld Freight plc Tel: 8537272

BUSINESS NEWS IN BRIEF

A large rise in the price of oil means that most freight rates will go up in the next few weeks. Newpoundland Railways say train fares will rise by 10% and National Trailers have already put up their prices by about 2p per kilometre.

The new container ship which is being built in Sutton Docks has brought employment to thousands of workers in the area. Many of the same people were made unemployed last year when the docks were containerised.

Counts Bank have said that they will charge customers from other banks who cash cheques at their branches. The charge will be 50p per cheque. The other major banks are considering whether to charge Counts' customers for the same service.

The Lutine Bell rang at Lloyd's when the SS Titania sank in the North Atlantic. Fortunately the Arctic Queen was near by and picked up all the crew. No one was killed. Underwriters will have to pay about £1m compensation. Transworld will handle some of the claims on behalf of their customers.

West Trucks Ltd have bought two dozen 'super trailers' from a mystery company. They did not name their suppliers who are in Belgium. Transworld do a lot of business with West Trucks, so we hope our customers' goods will travel on the super trailers which are faster and can carry heavier loads than standard trailers.

Don't forget the post code. That's the message from the post office. The postal system is now fully computerised and post without a post code will take longer to reach its destination. This is how the post code is made up:

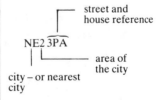

street and house reference

NE2 3PA

area of the city

city – or nearest city

London post codes begin with the area of London: SW (South West), WC (West Central) etc.

Exercise A *Business News*

Read 'Business news in Brief' and then listen to the Business News Headlines on the tape. How many differences can you find?

Unit Six
Distribution

📼 **Sandra Parr is giving Kevin Hughes his telephone messages.**

1 Hello, Sandra. Did anyone phone while I was out?

2 Yes. I've taken these messages for you.

MESSAGE: **1**

Can he send a container to Turin by trailer?

Taken by: Sandra
Date: Time: 9.30

MESSAGE: **2**

Do we carry live animals?

Taken by: Sandra
Date: Time: 9.42

---

3 Is it cheaper to send goods to Hamburg by road or rail?

Taken by: Sandra
Date: Time: 9.45

---

4 Can we collect goods from their factory?

Taken by:
Date: Time:

---

5 Do we handle containers?

Taken by: Sandra
Date: Time: 10.45

---

6 What are our European trailer charges?

Taken by: Anne
Date: Time: 10.34

Exercise 6.1 *Listening comprehension*

Listen to the tape and decide which person from which company asked which question in the telephone messages:

PEOPLE		COMPANIES	
Mr Grey	Mr Black	Dyers	Prism & Co
Mr White	Miss Green	Spectrum	Rainbow Co Ltd
Mrs Scarlet	Ms Brown	Tanners	Colourco

Exercise 6.2 *Reported questions*

Write about the questions people asked from the messages in Exercise 6.1, like this:

Can he send a container to Turin by trailer?
He asked whether he could send a container to Turin by trailer.

> *Laboratory drill*
> P: Can I send a container to Turin?
> R: *He asked whether he could send a container to Turin.*

Exercise 6.3 *Flight information*

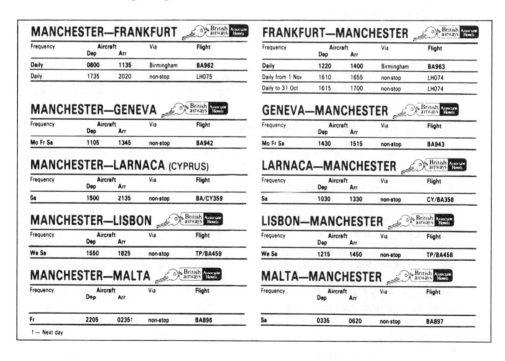

In pairs, request and give information about flights, like this:

P: *Could you tell me what time the BA962 leaves from Manchester?*
R: *Oh eight hundred. That's eight o'clock in the morning.*
P: *And what time does it arrive in Frankfurt?*
R: *1135. That's twenty-five to twelve local time.*

Laboratory drill A
P: Oh eight hundred

R: *That's eight o'clock in the morning.*

Laboratory drill B
P: Eight o'clock in the morning

R: *That's oh eight hundred on the 24-hour clock.*

Exercise 6.4   *Dictation*

 Listen to the tape and write down the questions people asked, like this:

1 *What time is the flight to Germany?*

Exercise 6.5   *Telephone enquiries*

In pairs, take your information from the Transworld brochure opposite and hold telephone conversations, like this:

P: *Transworld. Can I help you?*
R: *Could you tell me whether you've got a branch in Australia?*
P: *Yes. There's one in Sydney.*
R: *How can I get in touch with your Sydney office?*
P: *I'll give you their telex number. Have you got a pencil?*
R: *Yes.*
P: *It's 82659 AA.*
R: *Thanks very much.*

Laboratory drill

P: Australia

R: *Could you tell me whether you've got a branch in Australia?*

P: Yes. There's one in Sydney.

R: *How can I get in touch with your Sydney office?*

Exercise 6.6   *Reported questions*

In threes, take your information from the Transworld brochure and make enquiries and report questions as if the enquirer is on the phone, like this:

P: *Do you arrange transportation?*
R1: *What did he want to know?*
R2: *Whether we arranged transportation.*
P: *Can you store goods?*
R1: *What did she want to know?*
R2: *Whether we could store goods.*

Laboratory drill A
P: Ask them whether they arrange
   transportation.

R: *Do you arrange transportation?*

Laboratory drill B
P: Do you arrange transportation?
R: *He wanted to know whether we arranged transportation.*

Exercise 6.7   *Telephone conversations*

In pairs, act out some or all of the six conversations between Sandra/Anne and the callers from Exercise 6.1. Take your information from the telephone messages.

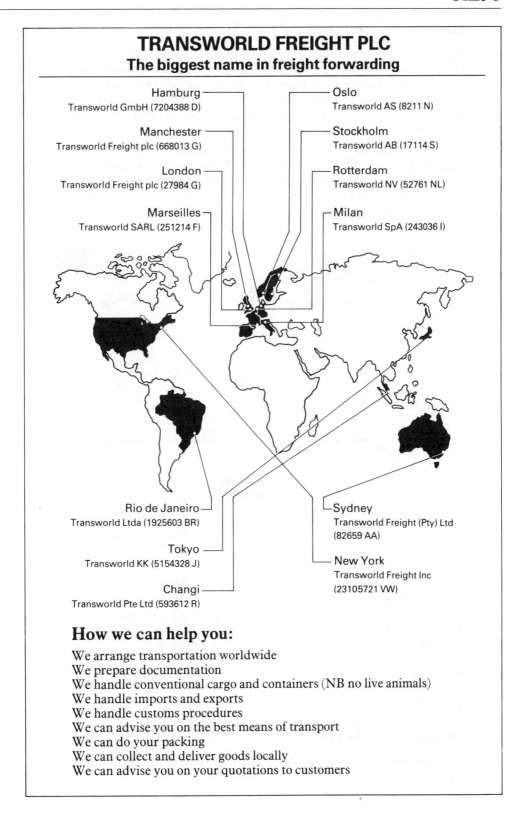

TRANSWORLD FREIGHT PLC
The biggest name in freight forwarding

Hamburg
Transworld GmbH (7204388 D)

Oslo
Transworld AS (8211 N)

Manchester
Transworld Freight plc (668013 G)

Stockholm
Transworld AB (17114 S)

London
Transworld Freight plc (27984 G)

Rotterdam
Transworld NV (52761 NL)

Marseilles
Transworld SARL (251214 F)

Milan
Transworld SpA (243036 I)

Rio de Janeiro
Transworld Ltda (1925603 BR)

Sydney
Transworld Freight (Pty) Ltd
(82659 AA)

Tokyo
Transworld KK (5154328 J)

New York
Transworld Freight Inc
(23105721 VW)

Changi
Transworld Pte Ltd (593612 R)

How we can help you:

We arrange transportation worldwide
We prepare documentation
We handle conventional cargo and containers (NB no live animals)
We handle imports and exports
We handle customs procedures
We can advise you on the best means of transport
We can do your packing
We can collect and deliver goods locally
We can advise you on your quotations to customers

Unit 6

Exercise 6.8   *Distribution of manufactured goods*

Manufacturers produce finished goods from raw materials or from components.
The places where they produce the goods are called factories. When they sell
the goods on the domestic market, they usually sell them in bulk to a
wholesaler. The wholesaler supplies the goods to many different retailers and
then the retailers sell them to individual customers. Companies usually store
goods in bulk in warehouses until they sell them.

Sometimes manufacturers, wholesalers or retailers export goods to wholesalers,
retailers or manufacturers in other countries. Sometimes they import goods from
other countries. A freight forwarder (or forwarding agent) is a company which
arranges the transportation of goods to and from other countries. Anyone who
sells goods abroad is an exporter. Anyone who buys goods from abroad is an
importer.

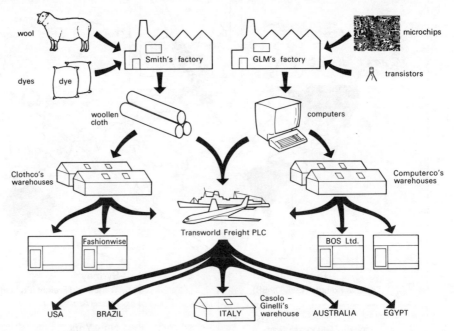

Match the names on the left with the words on the right:

1	wool and dyes	a	manufacturer
2	Smith's	b	freight forwarder
3	woollen cloth, computers	c	raw materials
4	Clothco	d	retailer
5	BOS Ltd	e	importer
6	transistors and microchips	f	wholesaler
7	Transworld Freight plc	g	components
8	Casolo-Ginelli	h	finished goods

Exercise 6.9   *The passive*

Processes and procedures are often described in the passive. Rewrite the first paragraph
of the text in Exercise 6.8 in the passive, starting like this:

Finished goods are produced from raw materials or from components.

> *Laboratory drill*
> P: They produce finished goods from raw materials.
> R: *Finished goods are produced from raw materials.*

Exercise 6.10 *Word puzzle*

Use the clues to help you complete this word puzzle. All the words are from Exercise 6.8.

Clues

1 Things from which goods are made which have not already been manufactured.
2 This person buys from the manufacturer and sells to the retailer
3 In large quantities
4 To give or send goods to someone
5 A place where goods are made
6 A shop which sells goods to individual customers
7 To make
8 If you sell goods in the country where they are produced, you sell them on the . . .
9 A place where goods and raw materials are stored in bulk
10 A person or company selling goods abroad
11 The parts of which finished goods are made
12 A forwarding agent

Hidden word: A person or company producing goods

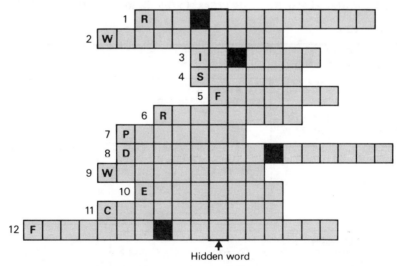

Hidden word

Exercise 6.11 *Oral (and written) presentation*

Prepare to talk for about two minutes about any of these four subjects:

1 The manufacture of Smith's woollen cloth and its distribution on the home market
2 The manufacture of Smith's woollen cloth and its distribution on the foreign market
3 The manufacture of GLM's computers and their distribution on the domestic market
4 The manufacture of GLM's computers and their distribution on the overseas market

Students take turns to name any other student and say which of the four subjects he/she must talk about. Afterwards write a paragraph about one of the subjects.

Exercise 6.12 *Requesting information in a letter*

Rewrite these questions as if they were in a letter of enquiry, like this:

How long does the journey to Australia take by sea?
I would be grateful if you could tell me how long the journey to Australia takes by sea.

1 What are your freight rates?
2 How much does it cost to send a small package airfreight?
3 What sort of packing is necessary for typewriters?
4 Where is the nearest airport to Cannes?
5 What time will the ship arrive in Manchester?
6 How big are standard containers?
7 How long does it take to send goods by air to Greece?
8 What time does the morning flight leave for Tokyo?

Exercise 6.13 *Telexing flight information*

Write answers to telexes (1) and (3) and the telex to which (2) is an answer. Take your information from the timetable in Exercise 6.3. Lay out your telexes properly with the correct answer back codes etc. Note:

a telexes are written in capital letters
b if you want an answer to your telex, write ?+ at the end
c if you do not want an answer to your telex, write + at the end

```
TRANSWLD 668013 G                                    1
GLM ENGING 22819 G       HALIFAX 11/04 1430

ATTN LONG

PLS INFORM DEPARTURE TIME AND FREQUENCY BA 962
MANCHESTER FRANKFURT VIA BIRMINGHAM?+

REGARDS STORKE


GLM ENGING 22819 G
TRANSWLD 668013 G
```

```
BOS 81259 G                                          2
TRANSWLD 668013 G        MANCHESTER 11/04 1600

ATTN BAKER

TP/BA 458 LISBON MANCHESTER ARRIVES 1450 WED AND SAT+

REGARDS LONG


TRANSWLD 668013 G
BOS 81259 G
```

```
TRANSWLD 668013 G
CYPRUS IMP 5138 CY       LARNACA  11/04  1612

ATTN LONG

PLS INFORM ARRIVAL TIME BOS ORDER 06325?+

REGARDS PASSAS


CYPRUS IMP 5138 CY
TRANSWLD 668013 G                                    3
```

Language notes

Reported questions (also called indirect questions)

The tense changes in reported questions are the same as those in reported speech (see Unit 3 language notes).

YES/NO QUESTIONS

'Is Anne going?'   *He asked whether Anne was going.*
'Did she meet John?'   *He wanted to know whether she had met John.*

QUESTION-WORD QUESTIONS

'Where does he live?'   *She asked where he lived.*
'What time is it?'   *She wanted to know what time it was.*

NB   We do not use inverted commas or question marks in reported questions.

The passive

The passive is often used when the person who does an action is unknown or not as important as what is done or what it is done to. The passive is formed with the verb *to be* (in all tenses) + past participle.

Someone is packing the goods.   *The goods are being packed.*
Someone packs the goods.   *The goods are packed.*
Someone packed the goods.   *The goods were packed.*
Someone has packed the goods.   *The goods have been packed.*
Someone will pack the goods.   *The goods will be packed.*
Someone is going to pack the goods.   *The goods are going to be packed.*

If the person who does the action is mentioned, we use *by*, eg *The goods were packed by Anne.* This usually emphasises who did the action

Telling the time

THE TWELVE-HOUR CLOCK

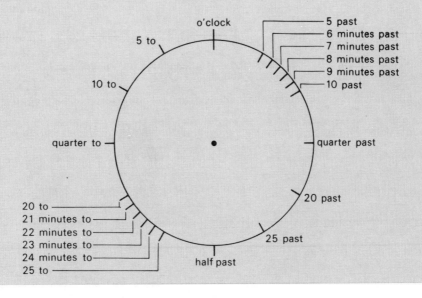

Unit 6

THE TWENTY-FOUR-HOUR CLOCK

1030   *ten thirty   (half past ten)*
1315   *thirteen fifteen   (quarter past one)*
1200   *twelve hundred   (twelve o'clock)*
0800   *oh eight hundred   (eight o'clock)*
0201   *two oh one   (one minute past two)*

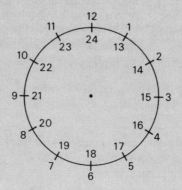

British English	American English
Note the spelling of *colour* in *Colourco.*	Note the spelling of *color.*
Enquiry or *inquiry* is pronounced /ɪnˈkwaɪərɪ/	*Inquiry* is pronounced /ˈɪnkwərɪ/

Unit Seven
Foreign Exchange

 At Transworld, Anne Bell and Sandra Parr are talking about holidays.

1 Are those holiday brochures?

Yes

2 What are you doing?

3 I can't afford to go to the continent now.

4 If the pound's weak though, more foreigners will buy British goods.

5 And if the economy improves, the pound will be strong again.

6 Get the brochures out of the bin!

Unit 7

Exercise 7.1   *Listening comprehension*

Listen to the tape and give short answers to these questions:
1   Where did Anne put the brochures?
2   Which 'continent' do you think Anne wanted to go to?
3   If your currency is weak, can you buy more or less foreign currency?
4   If your currency is strong, will more or fewer foreigners buy your country's goods?
5   If there is inflation, do prices go up or down?
6   Does *improve* mean (a) get better or (b) get worse?

Exercise 7.2   *An economic model*

This diagram shows a simplified view of a country's economy. Write notes to complete the other half of the diagram, like this:

a   *Spanish prices more expensive for foreigners*

NB   Which words are usually omitted in notes (and in telexes)?

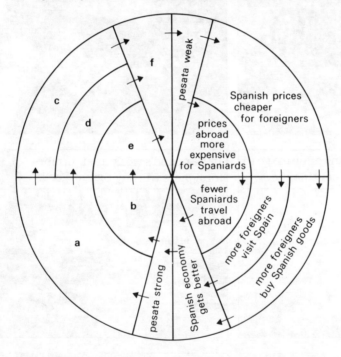

Exercise 7.3   *First conditional*

In pairs, discuss the economic model in Exercise 7.2, like this:

P: *What will happen if Spanish prices are cheap for foreigners?*
R: *More foreigners will buy Spanish goods and more foreigners will visit Spain.*

Laboratory drill A
P: What will happen if prices abroad are more expensive for Spaniards?
R: *Fewer Spaniards will travel abroad.*

Laboratory drill B
P: Will fewer Spaniards travel abroad?
R: *Yes, if prices abroad are more expensive for Spaniards.*

Exercise 7.4   *A view of the economy*

Read this paragraph about the diagram in Exercise 7.2, then write a similar paragraph about the second half of the diagram.

If the peseta is weak, Spanish prices will be cheaper for foreigners and prices abroad will be more expensive for Spaniards. This means that fewer Spaniards will travel abroad and more foreigners will visit Spain. It also means that more foreigners will buy Spanish goods, so the Spanish economy will improve and the peseta will be strong again.

Exercise 7.5   *International trade figures*

This table shows the trading figures between five countries for the year ending April 1983. The figures show the amount each country spent in thousands of pounds (eg S spent £225,000 on computers). The year each country started buying the goods or services is shown in brackets (eg V started selling computers to S in 1980).

In pairs, imagine you are journalists interviewing government ministers and talk about when the countries started trading, like this:

P: *Minister S. Could you tell us when tourists from your country started going to X?*
R: *In 1981. Two years ago.*[*]
P: *Minister W. Could you tell us the value of your exports to S?*
R: *Two hundred thousand pounds.*
P: *Minister V. Could you tell us when your country started trading with S?*
R: *In 1965. Eighteen years ago.*[*]

[*]These figures are correct for 1983. Change the number of years according to when you are using this book.

V	S	X	Y	W
sells computers to	(1980) 225	—	(1981) 100	(1978) 600
(1965) 300	exports meat to	(1975) 100	—	—
(1979) 100	(1981) 100	tourists come from	(1982) 50	(1980) 300
(1978) 100	(1968) 25	(1977) 25	sells insurance to	—
(1977) 600	(1978) 200	(1980) 300	(1979) 100	exports oil to

Laboratory drill
P: We sell computers

R: *Could you tell us when you started selling computers?*

Unit 7

Exercise 7.6   *Present perfect progressive*

In pairs, imagine you are journalists interviewing government ministers. Take your information from the table in Exercise 7.5 and talk about how long countries have been trading, like this:

P: *Excuse me, Minister V. I understand you sell computers to S?*
R: *Yes. We've been selling to S since 1980.*
or   *Yes. We've been selling to S for three years.**

*See note to Exercise 7.5.

Laboratory drill A
P: We sell computers
R: *How long have you been selling them?*

Laboratory drill B
P: You started selling to S in 1980.
R: *Yes. We've been selling to S since 1980.*
P: You started selling to S three years ago.
R: *Yes. We've been selling to S for three years.*

Exercise 7.7   *Visible and invisible imports and exports*

Goods, such as cloth and televisions, are visible (you can see them). Goods you sell abroad are visible exports. When you sell visible exports, money will come into your country. When you buy visible imports, money will leave your country.

Some imports and exports are invisible. For example, if an engineering expert from Country A goes to Country B to help them improve their engineering industry, he will earn money from B and bring it back to A. The expert is providing a service (which is his knowledge or expertise). For B this is an invisible import (because money leaves the country), but for A it is an invisible export (because money comes into the country).

Consider these situations and decide whether you are talking about visible imports, visible exports, invisible imports or invisible exports.

1   V sells computers to S. For V this is . . . . . .
2   V sells computers to S. For S this is . . . . . .
3   S sells meat to X. For S this is . . . . . .
4   Tourists go from Y to X. For X this is . . . . . .
5   Tourists come to X from V. For V this is . . . . . .
6   Y sells insurance to S. For S this is . . . . . .
7   X pays insurance premiums to Y. For Y this is . . . . . .
8   V buys oil from W. For W this is . . . . . .

Exercise 7.8   *Balance of Trade and Balance of Payments*

 The difference between the amount a country spends on visible imports and the amount it receives for visible exports is its Balance of Trade. The difference between the total amount a country spends, on imports (both visible and invisible) and other payments abroad, and the total amount it receives, from exports (both visible and invisible) and other receipts, is its Balance of Payments.

Take your information from the table in Exercise 7.5 and work out which figures are missing from the chart (to replace the letters a to n). Check your answers by listening to the tape.

| COUNTRY | VISIBLE | | BALANCE OF TRADE | INVISIBLE | | BALANCE OF PAYMENTS |
	IMPORTS	EXPORTS		IMPORTS	EXPORTS	
V	+900	+925	+25	−200	—	−175
S	a	b	−25	+125	c	−150
X	d	e	−400	f	g	+125
Y	h	—	−200	i	j	−100
W	k	l	+600	m	n	+300

Exercise 7.9   *Favourable and unfavourable balances*

In pairs, discuss the economy of each country, like this:
P: *Is V's Balance of Trade favourable or unfavourable?*
R: *It's favourable.*
P: *Does V have a Balance of Payments surplus or deficit?*
R: *A deficit.*

NB   Good (a plus figure) = favourable, a surplus; bad (a minus figure) = unfavourable, a deficit

Exercise 7.10   *A letter of enquiry*

Write to this hotel abroad asking for further information.
In the first paragraph say:
— where you saw the advertisement
— who is interested in staying at the hotel (invent a family for yourself if you like)
— when you are likely to come and for how long
In the second paragraph ask for more information, for example about
— the activities
— the price
— what meals and activities the price includes
— reductions in price for children
— how to get there

INTERNATIONAL SUN   13 April 1983

CLASSIFIED ADVERTISEMENTS

ACTIVITY HOLIDAYS for British and overseas families in NE England. Learn English by taking part in activities such as horse-riding, water-sports, drama and craft workshops and organised trips to the cathedral city of Durham or the 'living' museum at Beamish. Write for details to Fairfield House, Stanhope, Co. Durham, DL13 2UR UK.

NB   If you visit the hotel will you be a visible/invisible import/export for your country?

Exercise 7.11 *Currency exchange*

Look at this extract from a 1983 newspaper in the invented country of Newpoundland. Choose the correct words in italics for the news article to make sense.

COMPARATIVE PRICES FOR NEWPOUNDLAND HOLIDAYMAKERS

If you have been holidaying at home for the past four years, these are the prices you have been paying for three standard holiday items:

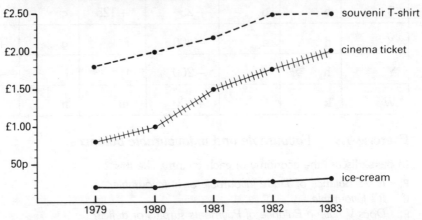

If you have been going to Dollardy for your holidays, this table shows the prices you have been paying:

Year	1979	1980	1981	1982	1983
Ice-cream	(40¢) 16p	(45¢) 18p	(50¢) 33p	(55¢) 22p	(60¢) 40p
Cinema ticket	($1.50) 60p	($2) 80p	($3) £2	($3.50) £1.40	($4.50) £3
T-shirt	($3.60) £1.36	($4) £1.60	($4.50) £3	($4.50) £1.80	($5) £3.33
Exchange rate £1 = $1 =	$2.50 40p	$2.50 40p	$1.50 66p	$2.50 40p	$1.50 66p

In a *1979/1983* you paid 20p for an ice-cream in this country, but this year you are paying b *30p/40p* for a similar ice-cream. The price rise is due to c *inflation/the exchange rate*. There has been inflation in d *Newpoundland/Dollardy* too. The price of an ice-cream there in e *1983/1979* was 40¢ and this year it is f *40¢/60¢*. However g *the exchange rate/inflation* has made a big difference to these prices for the Newpoundland tourist. In 1979 the value of the h *pound/dollar* was i *$1.50/$2.50*, so an ice-cream in j *Newpoundland/Dollardy* cost you k *16p/60p*. That was 4p l *more/less* than in Newpoundland. Today your m *dollar/pound* is only worth $1.50, so an ice-cream will cost you the equivalent of n *40p/40¢* – and that's o *10p/10¢* more than you are paying in Newpoundland. The message is clear. While the pound is p *weak/strong* Newpoundlanders should spend their holidays at home this year.

Exercise 7.12   *Oral presentation*

Prepare yourself to talk for one or two minutes about any of the comparative figures in the graph and table in Exercise 7.11, giving reasons for the differences and saying what the figures mean for people living in and travelling between Newpoundland and Dollardy. Students take turns to name any other student to talk about prices in a particular year or to compare the price of one item in two different years, for example:

– *Talk about the price of ice-cream and cinema tickets in Newpoundland and Dollardy in 1981.*
– *Talk about the comparative price of cinema tickets in Newpoundland and Dollardy in 1980 and 1982.*

Language notes

First conditional

We use the first conditional when something now or in the future is a possible or probable consequence of something else. It is made up of two clauses, the *if* clause (*if* + present tense) and the main clause (future or modal verb).

POSITIVE   *If it rains, we'll stay at home.*
            If the pound is strong, fewer people will visit England.
            If you work hard, you might go to university.

NB   The main clause can come before the *if* clause (without a comma) with no change of meaning: *We'll stay at home if it rains.*

QUESTION   *What will you do if it rains?*
            If the pound is strong, what will happen?
            Will you stay at home if it rains?
NEGATIVE   *If it does not rain, we'll go out.*
            If it is fine, we won't stay at home.
            If it isn't fine, we won't go out.
            We won't stay at home if it doesn't rain.
SHORT ANSWER   *Yes I will. No he won't.*

Present perfect progressive tense (also called the present perfect continuous)

The present perfect progressive is used for actions or states which began in the past and which are still happening. It is formed from the present tense of *have* + *been* + verb-*ing*.

POSITIVE   *He has been waiting since three o'clock.*
            We have been selling oil to Veland for 20 years.
QUESTION   *Have you been waiting long?*
            How long have you been waiting?
NEGATIVE   *I haven't been waiting long.*
SHORT ANSWER   *Yes I have. No he hasn't.*

Certain verbs already contain the idea of progression or continuity eg *be, own, possess, know*. These verbs are not usually used in the progressive tenses, so we say *I've owned the house since 1973*.
The two common verbs *live* and *work* can be used with either the progressive or the simple tense, so *I've lived/worked in London for 10 years*, and *I've been living/working in London for 10 years* are equally acceptable.

Unit Eight
Borrowing Money

 Anne Bell has just received a letter from her bank. She is telling Sandra Parr about it.

1 Oh no. I'm in the red.

2 I haven't heard that expression before.

3 I'll have to pay interest.

4 Is that very expensive?

5 Not usually as expensive as a loan, I suppose.

6 Is there an expression that means you're not overdrawn?

Exercise 8.1   *Listening comprehension*

Listen to the tape and choose the correct word to complete these statements.

1 If you are in the (*black*/*red*), your account is overdrawn.
2 If you have got an overdraft, you have not got any money in your
   (*account*/*statement*).
3 The amount that is overdrawn used to be written in red on your bank
   (*account*/*statement*).
4 The bank (*charges*/*pays*) you interest if your account is overdrawn.
5 Interest is what you (*pay*/*receive*) for borrowing money.
6 A loan is usually (*more*/*less*) expensive than an overdraft.
7 If your account is (*in credit*/*overdrawn*) you will be charged interest.
8 When you have got money in your account, you are 'in the black'.

Exercise 8.2   *Comparatives*

In pairs, pretend to misunderstand these statements and correct yourselves using
comparatives, like this:

> P: *An overdraft is usually cheaper than a loan.*
> R: *Oh, so a loan is cheaper.*
> P: *No. A loan isn't as cheap!*

1 The first invoice was higher than the second.
2 PDT's goods are more expensive than GLM's.
3 BOS's delivery is quicker than PDT's.
4 BOS's prices are lower than GTG's.
5 Smiths' cloth is better than Jones'.

Laboratory drill
P: An overdraft is usually cheaper than a loan.   R: *So a loan is cheaper.*
P: No.   R: *So a loan isn't as cheap.*

Exercise 8.3   *Calculations*

In pairs, say and work out these calculations, like this:

> 5×4 P: *Five multiplied by four*
>   R: *Five multiplied by four equals twenty.*

a $6 \div 2$ f $12 + 5$
b $8 + 9$ g $23 - 2$
c $30 - 6$ h $99 \div 9$
d $20 \div 2$ i 20×4
e 7×3 j $40 + 11$

Laboratory drill
P: Five multiplied by four   R: *Twenty*

Unit 8

Exercise 8.4   *Borrowing money*

Kevin *borrowed* £3,600 from the bank to buy a car. In other words:

Kevin had a *loan* from the bank.
The bank *lent* Kevin £3,600.
Kevin had a *debt* of £3,600.
Kevin *owed* the bank £3,600.
Kevin is the bank's *debtor*.
The bank is Kevin's *creditor*.

Kevin is *repaying* the loan over three years and he is paying *interest* on the loan at the rate of 10% per annum on a decreasing balance. In other words, in the first month he repaid £100 *capital* and £30 *interest* (10% × £3,600/12 months). In the second month, the *balance* on his capital repayment was £3,500 (£3,600 − £100 he repaid in the first month), so he repaid £100 capital and £29.25 interest (10% × £3,500/12 months).

Anne had a loan of £600 from the bank. She paid it back over twelve months at a rate of 10% pa on a decreasing balance.

In pairs, ask and answer questions about Anne's loan using the words in italics in the text above, like this:

P: *How much money did Anne borrow?*
R: *£600*

Exercise 8.5   *Definitions*

In small groups, student's take turns to define these words and other students say which words have been defined, like this:

P: *Your account is in the red. In other words, your account is ......*
R: *Overdrawn*

a	statement	f	per annum	k	overdrawn
b	borrow	g	interest	l	in credit
c	repay	h	balance	m	overdraft
d	debtor	i	creditor	n	transaction
e	per cent	j	account	o	capital

> *Laboratory drill*
> P: Your account is in the red. In other words, your account is ......
> R: *Overdrawn*

Exercise 8.6   *Word stress*

Divide the words in Exercise 8.5 into syllables and decide where you think the main stress is, like this:

a   statement   *state-ment*   *STATE-ment*

Listen to the words on the tape to check your answers.

64

Exercise 8.7 *Articles*

Decide whether each gap in this passage should be filled with *a* or *the*.

There are two main kinds of international plastic cards. ¹..*The* first kind are travel and entertainment cards such as American Express, Diner's Club and Carte Blanche. ²..*The* second kind are Visa and Mastercard credit cards which have different local names in each country. In Britain ³..*the* former is called Barclaycard and ⁴..*the* latter is called Access.

Both sorts of cards can be used in many hotels, restaurants and shops worldwide. When ⁵...... cardholder pays ⁶...... bill, ⁷...... details are written on ⁸...... sales voucher, which ⁹..*the* cardholder signs. ¹⁰...... shop or restaurant gives ¹¹...... top copy to ¹²..*the* customer, sends ¹³...... copy to ¹⁴...... finance company and keeps ¹⁵...... copy. ¹⁶..*the* finance company pays ¹⁷...... shop ¹⁸...... amount of ¹⁹...... bill, but takes off ²⁰..*a* small percentage charge. For example, if ²¹...... bill is £60, ²²..*the* finance company takes off 5% and pays ²³..*the* shop £57. ²⁴..*The* finance company sends every cardholder ²⁵..*a* statement each month with details of all ²⁶..*the* transactions in that month.

Travel and entertainment card accounts must be paid in full every month. Credit cardholders do not have to pay their accounts every month, but they must pay a minimum amount of £5 or 5% of the bill (whichever is greater). Then ²⁷..*the* outstanding balance, plus interest, is written on ²⁸..*the* next statement.

Cardholders pay for travel and entertainment cards (²⁹..*the* annual subscription for both American Express and Diner's Club is £17.50), but credit cards are free in Britain.

N.B.   In Britain some credit cards are also cheque cards. Barclaycard guarantees cheques drawn on Barclays Bank and Access guarantees cheques drawn on ³⁰...... National Westminster Bank.

Exercise 8.8 *Note-taking*

Replace the letters A to N in this table with answers taken from the text in Exercise 8.7.

	AMERICAN EXPRESS	BARCLAYCARD VISA
Is it a travel and entertainment card?	A	B
Is it a credit card?	C	D
How much does it cost the cardholder?	E	F
What is the minimum repayment each month?	G	H
Can the cardholder get credit?	I	J
Does the cardholder pay interest?	K	L
Is it a cheque card?	M	N

Unit 8

Exercise 8.9   *The former/the latter*

The former means the first one of two or three. *The latter* means the last one of two or three. Rewrite these sentences, like this:

The two credit cards are Visa and Mastercard. Visa is called Barclaycard and Mastercard is called Access.
The former is called Barclaycard and the latter is called Access.

1   There was a group of men and a group of women. The men were French and the women were German.
2   There are two specialised kinds of consignment note called an air waybill and a Bill of Lading. One is for goods sent by sea and the other is for goods sent by air.
3   There are travel and entertainment cards and credit cards. Access is an example of a credit card.
4   There are credit cards and travel entertainment cards. You pay a subscription for travel and entertainment cards. Credit cards are free.
5   Here is an order and an invoice. One of them is a request for payment. The other is a request for goods.

Exercise 8.10   *Oral (and written) presentation*

Prepare a short talk (one or two minutes) on all of the following topics:
1   Mastercards
2   Credit cards
3   Travel and entertainment cards
4   Diner's Club cards
5   Cheque cards
In small groups, students take turns to name another student and say which topic he/she should talk about. Students can refer to notes, but should not write out their talk.
Write a paragraph about one of the subjects.

Exercise 8.11   *A bank statement*

The answers to this puzzle are all numbers taken from the statement. One of the numbers is already filled in for you.

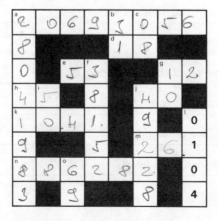

```
BONDS BANK plc                STATEMENT
CITY BRANCH                   OF ACCOUNT


MS A BELL                     20693056
69 MAPLE ROAD
MANCHESTER M3 2BY             28 APR 83


                             1983/4
                             debit    credit
```

Customer's Notes	Details	Payments	Receipts	Date	Balance
	BALANCE FORWARD		be've'kl	28 MAR	70.76DR
Cash	886277	40.00		29 MAR	110.76DR
Paycheque	REMITTANCE		492.28	29 MAR	381.52
	INTEREST	.32			381.20
Rent	886276	120.00		31 MAR	261.20
Insurance premium	886279	85.20		1 APR	176.00
Barclaycard	886278	53.67		8 APR	
Supermarket	886280	10.41		9 APR	
Cash	886281	45.00		12 APR	66.92
Tel. bill	886283	35.00		19 APR	
Cash.	886282	50.00		20 APR	18.10DR

```
        OVERDRAWN BALANCE IS INDICATED BY THE LETTERS DR
```

Clues across
a Anne Bell's a/c number
d The number of pounds Anne was overdrawn on 20 April
e The number of pounds Anne paid to Barclaycard
g On this day £45 was deducted from the account
h The amount Anne took out with cheque number 886281
j The first amount of cash Anne took out
k The amount Anne paid to the supermarket
m The number of pounds in the a/c on 31 March
n This cheque was written before the telephone bill, but deducted from the account after it

Clues down
a The date of the statement
b On this day the balance was £261.20
c On this day the balance was £122.33
f The balance on 29 March
g The number of pence Anne was overdrawn on 20 April
i The last transaction on this statement was for ......
j The amount Anne paid into the account
l The balance on this date was £176
m The number of pounds in the account on 31 March
o The number of Anne's house

Unit 8

Exercise 8.12   *Punctuation*

Rewrite this letter with the necessary punctuation and capital letters.

```
                                                bonds bank plc
                                                city branch
                                                25 high street
                                                manchester m1 2aa


         ms a bell
         69 maple road
         manchester m3 2by                       20 april 1983



         dear ms bell

         i am sorry to inform you that your account is overdrawn
         by £18.10 i would not usually bother about such a small
         amount but you regularly overdraw your account at the
         end of each month without informing us i would be grateful
         if you would come in to talk to me about this as soon
         as possible

         yours sincerely

         terence gregory mr
         manager
```

Language notes

Articles

DEFINITE ARTICLE   *The* (pronounced /ðə/ before a consonant and /ði/ or /ði:/ before a vowel) is used:

1   before nouns when there is only one
    the earth, the sun
2   when we know which thing(s) or person/people is/are being talked about
    the boys in the corner, the top copy of the bill
3   in superlatives to express comparison
    He is the tallest.
4   in dates in the spoken form
    the 25th of May, January the 23rd
5   before the names of ships
    the Australian Queen
6   before the names of certain countries
    the United States (but *America*), *the Netherlands* (but *Holland*), *the United Kingdom* (but *Great Britain*), *the USSR* (but *Russia*)

INDEFINITE ARTICLE   *A* (before a consonant, pronounced /ə/) or *an* (before a vowel or a silent h, pronounced /ən/) is used only before a singular count noun:

1   when it is mentioned for the first time and does not represent a particular person or thing
    Barclaycard is a credit card. She works in an office.
2   with professions, jobs
    He is a sales assistant.
3   with certain numerical expressions
    a dozen, a quarter, an eighth, a hundred
4   in expressions of price, speed or ratio (instead of *per*)
    50p a kilo (50p per kilo), 80 kilometres an hour
5   before the name of a person the speaker does not know
    A Mr Smith telephoned.

Capital letters

USE	EXAMPLE
names, titles and initials of people and companies	*Ms Anne Bell, Mr J Hyam Jr, Transworld Freight*
countries, nationalities	*Belgium, French*
places, rivers, mountains etc	*London, Hampshire, River Thames, Mount Everest*
days, months	*Monday, January*
at the beginning of a sentence	*Thank you for your letter.*
I	*I know him and I like him.*
with some documents and abbreviations	*Bill of Lading, L/C*
in telexes	*PLS SEND INVOICE*

Punctuation marks

	EXAMPLE
FULL STOP (US: PERIOD)	
at the end of a sentence	*He works at Transworld.*
in decimals, money	*562.3, £25.50, $6.75*
QUESTION MARK	
after a question	*Did you see him yesterday?*
NB not after reported questions	*I asked whether you'd seen him.*
COMMA	
before and/or after someone's name when you are writing to them	*Hello, Jane.* *What are you doing, Anne?*
in a list of several things	*She has got long, dark, curly hair.* *I went to London, Rome and Paris.*
in numbers over 999	*1,786,000*
before direct speech	*She said, 'Hello.'*
either side of a non-defining relative clause	*The invoice, which is a request for payment, is out-of-date*
before some clauses and conjunctions eg *but, so, then*	*If I see him, I'll tell him.* *I went into his office, but he wasn't there.*
NB not before *and, or*	*I went into his office and into her office.*

APOSTROPHE

Belonging to *Mary*	*Mary's office*
BOS	*BOS's staff* (or *BOS' staff*)
the manager	*the manager's books*
the managers	*the managers' books*

Short forms (contractions)   *I'll (I will), he isn't (he is not)*

INVERTED COMMAS/QUOTATION MARKS

with direct speech   *He said, 'She likes coffee.*

NB   not with reported speech   *He said she liked coffee.*

Calculations

$2 + 4 = 6$ Two $\begin{cases} plus \\ and \\ added\ to \end{cases}$ four $\begin{cases} equals \\ is \\ makes \end{cases}$ six

$9 - 7$ Nine $\begin{cases} minus \\ take\ away \end{cases}$ seven   Seven $\begin{cases} subtracted\ from \\ from \end{cases}$ nine

5×3 Five $\begin{cases} multiplied\ by \\ times \end{cases}$ three

$20 \div 4$ *Twenty divided by four*

| **British English** | **American English** |
| A sum of borrowed money is called *capital* | A sum of borrowed money is called *principal* |

Unit Nine
Computerised Accounts

 Sandra Parr is talking to Liz Shepherd about a letter that has just arrived.

1 Liz, a customer's sent us a cheque for no pounds and no pence.

2 What? Who?

Someone from BOS Ltd.

3 Oh, we can thank the computer for that.

4 It prints out a statement every month for our regular customers, even if they don't owe us money.

5 Why do you send them?

We don't usually,...

6 ...but David's new to the department. I'll have a word with him about it.

Unit 9

Exercise 9.1   *Corrections*

Listen to the tape and correct these statements, like this:

The letter was opened by ...... (name the correct person).

1   Someone at BOS opened the letter.
2   David Thompson printed the statement.
3   Liz Shepherd wrote the letter.
4   Sandra Parr sent the statement.
5   The computer wrote the letter of apology.

Laboratory drill
P: Sandra opened the letter.   R: *The letter was opened by Sandra.*

Exercise 9.2   *A letter*

Listen to the tape and write the letter that Sandra talked to Liz about. You can find the top of the letter in Exercise 9.9 (number 1). It was written by Mr Geoffrey Best.

Exercise 9.3   *Computers*

Many companies have now computerised their accounting procedures because computers can do the work more quickly and more accurately than people. The work the computer does (storing information, finding the right information and doing calculations) is called data processing. The part of the computer that processes the data (information) is called the CPU (central processing unit). This contains only electronic components, called microchips.

A computer can only do what it is instructed to do. The instructions that are stored in a computer are called the computer program. The people who write these instructions and put them in the computer are called computer programmers. You do not have to be a computer programmer to use a computer.

The parts of the computer that most people use are called terminals. The terminals are usually a keyboard, which looks like a typewriter, and a VDU (visual display unit), which looks like a television, or a printer. Information put into the computer on the keyboard is called input. When the computer shows the result of the data processing on the VDU or the printer, this is called output.

When computers go wrong, it is usually because there is something wrong with the input. In other words, it is a mistake made by a person, not by the computer. This is sometimes called GIGO (Garbage In, Garbage Out*).

*Garbage is the American word for *rubbish*, something you throw away because it is not any good.

Computers can only answer questions which require a positive or negative (yes or no) answer. In pairs, ask and answer this sort of question about the computer text, like this:

P: *Does data mean information?*   R: *Yes*
P: *Does a VDU look like a*   R: *No*
     typewriter?
P: *Where are the microchips?*   R: *Input error*

Laboratory drill
P: Does data mean information?   R: *Yes*
P: Where are the microchips?   R: *Input error*

Exercise 9.4   *Computer tape*

Different words are stored on these pieces of computer tape. Each series of holes always stands for the same letter. Use the clues to help you work out which words are stored. The first letter of each word is given to you.

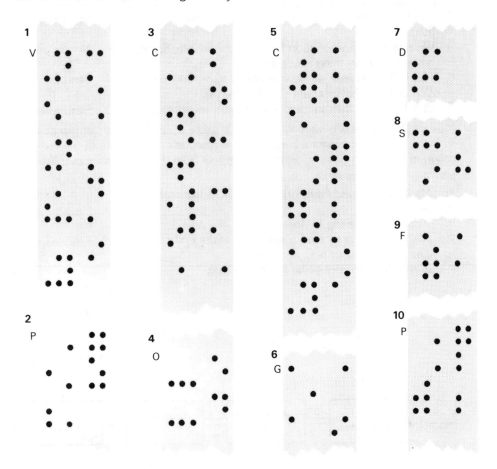

Clues

1   A computer terminal which looks like a television
2   The instructions written in a computer
3   VDUs, keyboards and printers are all . . . . . .
4   The information that comes out of a computer
5   The main part of a computer that contains microchips
6   This means that if you put the wrong input into a computer, you will get mistakes in the output
7   Information
8, 9 and 10   Three things a computer can do with information

Unit 9

Exercise 9.5   *A computer program*

David Thompson does not yet understand the documents used in the accounts department. This is the situation with six Transworld customers and what David was planning to do about them:

1 We haven't arranged transportation for BOS this month.

2 We arranged transportation for GLM and they have paid the invoice, but we overcharged them.

3 We arranged transportation for our regular customers, JLN, but they haven't paid us.

4 HEQ have paid their invoice, but we undercharged them.

5 We arranged transportation for WRS this month, but we haven't done anything about it yet.

6 This is the first time we have arranged transportation for ZYZ and they haven't paid their invoice yet.

7 BLT have paid their invoice. The amount was correct.

A Send a statement at the end of the month

B Send a credit note

C Send a debit note

D Send a reminder

E Not do anything

F Send an invoice

G Send a receipt

Most of David's answers were wrong, so Liz wrote a simple 'computer program' for him to follow. Study the program below, then in pairs, ask questions from the computer program and give a positive or negative answer from the problems above, like this:

P: *The customer is BOS.*
R: *Have we arranged transportation for BOS this month?*
P: *Negative*
R: *What are you going to do?*
P: *Well I was going to send a statement at the end of the month.*
R: *The correct answer is E.*
P: *In that case, I'm not going to do anything.*

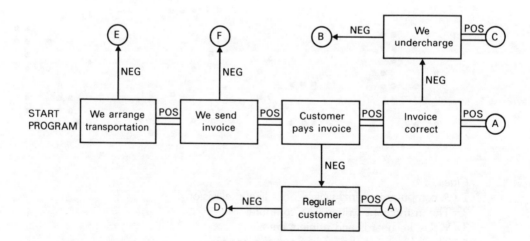

Laboratory drill
P: What about BOS's account?   R: *I was going to send a statement at the end of the month.*

74

Exercise 9.6 *The alphabet*

This is a list of new customers at Transworld. Put them in alphabetical order before they are put on the computer.

1	JBX Pte Ltd	7	ABD plc
2	JDR Inc .	8	GLM AB
3	WRS AS	9	VDU SpA
4	JLN GmbH	10	HEQ (Pty) Ltd
5	FPT Ltda	11	ZZY KK
6	BLT SARL	12	ZYZ NV

Check which country you think each company is in, like this:

P: *JBX is Singaporean, isn't it?* R: *Yes. It's in Singapore.*
or *No. It's in . . . . . .*

Laboratory drill A
P: One R: *JBX*

Laboratory drill B
P: JBX is Singaporean. R: *JBX is in Singapore, is it?*

Exercise 9.7 *A telephone conversation*

Rewrite the lines of this telephone conversation between Sandra and a caller in the right order. Decide who says which lines.

1 Could I speak to Mr Thompson please?
2 'Bye.
3 I'm afraid not. I've got a message that he's ill.
4 Good mor . . . or rather Good afternoon.
5 Transworld Freight. Good morning.
6 Not at all. Goodbye.
7 Er . . . Mr Thompson who works in the accounts department.
8 Oh. Is it after 12? Good afternoon.
9 Is that Mr David Thompson with a 'p' or Mr Jack Thomson?
10 Oh no. It's all right. Do you know when he'll be back?
11 Oh you want David Thompson. I'm afraid he's not at work today. Can I take a message?
12 Well I'll try again tomorrow. Thanks very much.

Exercise 9.8 *Information transfer*

Rewrite each of these sentences in two other ways, for example, if it is from a telex, rewrite it as if it is in a telephone conversation and in a formal business letter.

1 I am sorry to inform you that we have not received your remittance.
2 Please send us the order number as soon as you can.
3 REGRET CONSIGNMENT 8934 DAMAGED
4 We would be grateful if you could send the documents at your earliest convenience.
5 PLS SEND FLIGHT DETAILS SOONEST
6 I'm afraid the ship hasn't arrived yet.

Exercise 9.9 *In-tray exercise*

When Sandra arrived at work on 10 May, this was the correspondence she found on her desk. Read through it as quickly as possible and decide (as if you are Sandra) what you are going to do with it.

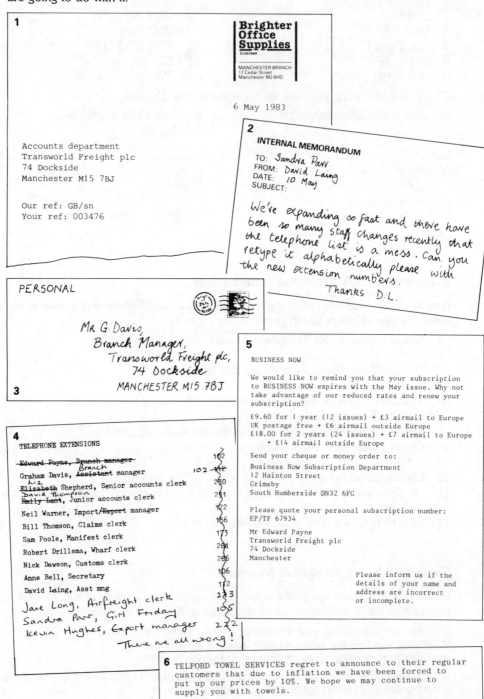

1

Brighter Office Supplies Limited

MANCHESTER BRANCH
17 Cedar Street
Manchester M2 6HD

6 May 1983

Accounts department
Transworld Freight plc
74 Dockside
Manchester M15 7BJ

Our ref: GB/sn
Your ref: 003476

2

INTERNAL MEMORANDUM

TO: Sandra Parr
FROM: David Laing
DATE: 10 May
SUBJECT:

We've expanding so fast and there have been so many staff changes recently that the telephone list is a mess. Can you retype it alphabetically please with the new extension numbers.
Thanks D.L.

3

PERSONAL

Mr G. Davis,
Branch Manager,
Transworld Freight plc,
74 Dockside
MANCHESTER M15 7BJ

4

TELEPHONE EXTENSIONS

~~Edward Payne, Branch manager~~   102
  Branch
Graham Davis, ~~Assistant~~ manager   102 112
  Liz
~~Elizabeth~~ Shepherd, Senior accounts clerk   280
  David Thompson
~~Emily Lant,~~ Junior accounts clerk   281
Neil Warner, Import/~~Export~~ manager   182
Bill Thomson, Claims clerk   156
Sam Poole, Manifest clerk   173
Robert Drillsma, Wharf clerk   284
Nick Dawson, Customs clerk   286
Anne Bell, Secretary   106
David Laing, Asst mng   112
Jane Long, Airfreight clerk   105
Sandra Parr, Girl Friday
Kevin Hughes, Export manager   222
  These are all wrong!

5

BUSINESS NOW

We would like to remind you that your subscription to BUSINESS NOW expires with the May issue. Why not take advantage of our reduced rates and renew your subscription?

£9.60 for 1 year (12 issues) + £3 airmail to Europe
UK postage free + £6 airmail outside Europe
£18.00 for 2 years (24 issues) + £7 airmail to Europe
     + £14 airmail outside Europe

Send your cheque or money order to:
Business Now Subscription Department
12 Hainton Street
Grimsby
South Humberside DN32 6FG

Please quote your personal subscription number:
EP/TF 67934

Mr Edward Payne
Transworld Freight plc
74 Dockside
Manchester

Please inform us if the details of your name and address are incorrect or incomplete.

6 TELFORD TOWEL SERVICES regret to announce to their regular customers that due to inflation we have been forced to put up our prices by 10%. We hope we may continue to supply you with towels.

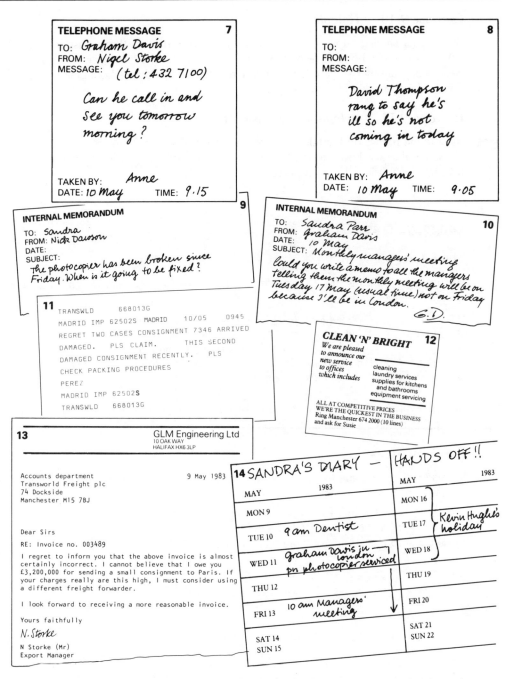

TELEPHONE MESSAGE 7

TO: *Graham Davis*
FROM: *Nigel Storke*
MESSAGE: *(tel : 432 7100)*

*Can he call in and
see you tomorrow
morning?*

TAKEN BY: *Anne*
DATE: *10 May* TIME: *9.15*

TELEPHONE MESSAGE 8

TO:
FROM:
MESSAGE:

*David Thompson
rang to say he's
ill so he's not
coming in today*

TAKEN BY: *Anne*
DATE: *10 May* TIME: *9.05*

INTERNAL MEMORANDUM 9

TO: *Sandra*
FROM: *Nick Dawson*
DATE:
SUBJECT:
*The photocopier has been broken since
Friday. When is it going to be fixed?*

INTERNAL MEMORANDUM 10

TO: *Sandra Parr*
FROM: *Graham Davis*
DATE: *10 May*
SUBJECT: *Monthly managers' meeting*
*Could you write a memo to all the managers
telling them the monthly meeting will be on
Tuesday 17 May (usual time) not on Friday
because I'll be in London.* *G.D.*

11

```
TRANSWLD      668013G
MADRID IMP 62502S MADRID   10/05    0945
REGRET TWO CASES CONSIGNMENT 7346 ARRIVED
DAMAGED.   PLS CLAIM.       THIS SECOND
DAMAGED CONSIGNMENT RECENTLY.   PLS
CHECK PACKING PROCEDURES
PEREZ
MADRID IMP 62502S
TRANSWLD      668013G
```

CLEAN 'N' BRIGHT 12

*We are pleased
to announce our
new service
to offices
which includes*
cleaning
laundry services
supplies for kitchens
and bathrooms
equipment servicing

ALL AT COMPETITIVE PRICES
WE'RE THE QUICKEST IN THE BUSINESS
Ring Manchester 674 2000 (10 lines)
and ask for Susie

13

GLM Engineering Ltd
10 OAK WAY
HALIFAX HX6 3LP

Accounts department   9 May 1983
Transworld Freight plc
74 Dockside
Manchester M15 7BJ

Dear Sirs
RE: Invoice no. 003489
I regret to inform you that the above invoice is almost
certainly incorrect. I cannot believe that I owe you
£3,200,000 for sending a small consignment to Paris. If
your charges really are this high, I must consider using
a different freight forwarder.

I look forward to receiving a more reasonable invoice.

Yours faithfully
N. Storke
N Storke (Mr)
Export Manager

14 SANDRA'S DIARY — HANDS OFF!!

MAY 1983	MAY 1983
MON 9	MON 16
TUE 10 *9 am Dentist*	TUE 17 *Kevin Hughes' holiday*
WED 11 *Graham Davis in London photocopier serviced*	WED 18
THU 12	THU 19
FRI 13 *10 am Managers' meeting*	FRI 20
SAT 14	SAT 21
SUN 15	SUN 22

In small groups, discuss (as if you were Sandra) what you are going to do about the post,
like this:

P: *What are you going to do about letter number 1?*

R: *I'm going to give it to Liz Shepherd in the accounts
department.*

P: { *Oh, you're right. I was going to answer it.*
    { *Yes. That's what I was going to do.*

Exercise 9.10   *Roleplay*

Still in your small groups, act out the conversations to do with the correspondence, either on the telephone or face-to-face. For example, for the first letter, one student is Sandra and another student is Liz Shepherd. Different students should take the part of Sandra for the different conversations.

Exercise 9.11   *Telephone extension list*

Rewrite the names on the telephone extension list (Exercise 9.9 number 4) in alphabetical order. Listen to the tape to check your order and write down the new telephone extensions for each person.

Language notes

The future: going to

We use *going to* + infinitive for an intention about the future before we have made any definite arrangements.

POSITIVE	*He's going to be a doctor when he grows up.*
QUESTION	*What are you going to do in the summer?*
	Is he going to leave Transworld, do you know?
NEGATIVE	*I'm not going to stay in Manchester for the rest of my life.*
SHORT ANSWER	*Yes I am. No he's not.*

NB *Going to* is not usually used with the verbs *come* and *go*. The present progressive is used instead eg *I'm going to Greece, I hope.*

Was/were going to

We use *was/were going to* + infinitive to express a past intention which may or may not still happen/have happened.

I was going to send an invoice, but I've changed my mind.
I was going to talk to Mary. – Oh, so was I. Let's go together.
I was going to visit Anne last night, but she was out.

Unit Ten
Types of Business

 David Thompson is talking to Liz Shepherd about the ownership of Transworld.

1 Liz, who owns Transworld?

I do.

2 You?

Well, I own a bit of it. Transworld is a public limited company. Anyone can buy shares.

3 So if I bought more shares than you, I could have your job?

4 If you bought more than 50% of the shares, you'd control the company.

5 Have you got fifty thousand pounds or so?

No. Why?

6 Because that's what a controlling interest in Transworld would cost you.

Unit 10

Exercise 10.1 *Listening comprehension*

Listen to the tape and decide whether (a) or (b) completes these sentences correctly.

1. PLC stands for (a) private limited company (b) public limited company.
2. Liz owns (a) part of Transworld (b) all of Transworld.
3. Shareholders are people who (a) work for the company (b) own part of the company.
4. Most people invest in public limited companies because (a) they work for the company (b) they want to make money.
5. To make a profit is (a) to earn money (b) to pay out money.
6. If you save money in a bank deposit account (a) the bank pays you interest (b) you pay the bank interest.
7. The money you make from owning shares is called (a) a dividend (b) interest.
8. If David owned more shares than Liz, he (a) probably would (b) probably would not get her job.
9. If you have a controlling interest in a company, you own (a) less than 50% of the shares (b) more than half the shares.
10. David (a) is going to (b) is not going to buy a controlling interest in Transworld.

Exercise 10.2 *Percentages and fractions*

In pairs, express these fractions as percentages, like this:

P: *How do you express a third as a percentage?*
R: *Thirty-three and a third per cent*

1 $\frac{1}{2}$	3 $\frac{2}{3}$	5 1	7 $\frac{1}{10}$	9 $\frac{4}{5}$
2 $\frac{1}{4}$	4 $\frac{3}{4}$	6 $\frac{1}{5}$	8 $\frac{9}{10}$	10 $\frac{1}{100}$

Laboratory drill A
P: A third
R: *Thirty-three and a third per cent*

Laboratory drill B
P: Thirty-three and a third per cent
R: *A third*

Exercise 10.3 *Setting up a limited company*

Derek, Roger, Malcolm and John have started a limited company in Britain.

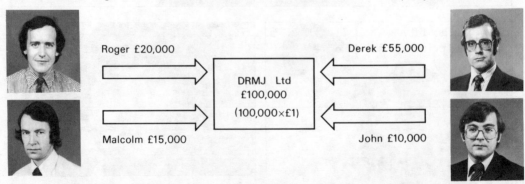

Roger £20,000 → DRMJ Ltd £100,000 (100,000×£1) ← Derek £55,000
Malcolm £15,000 → ← John £10,000

Derek, Roger, Malcolm and John are all investors and shareholders.
Roger invested £20,000. John put in £10,000.
Derek is the majority shareholder (he owns the most shares).

Derek also has a controlling interest (he owns more than 50% of the shares).
The company's capital (the money it has for buying goods and equipment) is
£100,000.
The company's capital is divided into 100,000 shares of £1 each.
£1 is the nominal value (or the par value, or the face value) of each share.
Malcolm owns 15,000 shares. The nominal value of his shares is £15,000.

After a year, the company makes £15,000 profit. This is divided between the
shareholders. The company announces a dividend of 15p per share (£15,000
profit ÷ 100,000 shares).
Malcolm received £2,250 (15,000 shares × 15p).

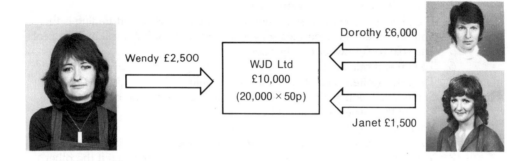

Profit after the first year = £1,000.

In pairs, ask and answer questions about WJD Ltd using the vocabulary above, like this:

P: *Who is the majority shareholder?*   R: *Dorothy*
P: *What is the par value of Janet's shares?*   R: *£1,500*

> *Laboratory drill*
> P: Who is the majority shareholder?   R: *Dorothy*

Exercise 10.4   *Investing in a limited company*

When a limited company has started trading, you do not invest in shares by
giving more capital to the company. You buy them from one of the shareholders.
If it is a private limited company, a shareholder can only sell shares if all the
other shareholders agree. If it is a public limited company, shares can be
bought and sold freely, usually at a Stock Exchange. If the company is doing
well and paying high dividends, then you might pay more than the face value of
the shares. If it is doing badly, you might pay less than the face value of the
shares. The price you pay at the Stock Exchange (or to a shareholder) for your
shares is their market value.

If the company fails, it will stop trading and go into liquidation. This means that
all the company's property and equipment (its assets) must be sold and the
money from the sale will be used to pay its debts to its creditors. The
shareholders may lose the money they paid for the shares. If the company still
does not have enough money to pay all its debts, the shareholders do not have
to pay any more money. In other words, the shareholders' liability for debts is
limited to the value of their shares.

On the other hand, if you are an owner of a business which is not limited, for example a sole proprietorship (owned by one person) or a partnership (owned by between 2 and 20 people) and your business fails, you will go bankrupt. In this case you might have to sell your own private possessions (your house, car, furniture etc) to pay all your creditors. In other words, sole proprietors and partners have unlimited liability for their firm's debts.

Use the clues to help you complete the puzzle. The words are all in the text on page 81 and above.

Clues

1. The money shareholders put into a company to buy property and equipment so it can start trading *capital*
2. One of the owners of a partnership
3. The price you pay for shares when the company has started trading is their . . . *market* value
4. To put money into a business or a bank account so that it will make a profit
5. The sole (only) owner of a business
6. To buy and sell goods
7. The price written on a share is its *face* value
8. Something belonging to a person or a business which can be sold
9. One of the owners of a limited company *shareholder*
10. Your legal duty to other people, eg to your creditors
11. If a sole proprietorship or a partnership fails, the owners will go . . . . . .
12. You can only buy or sell shares in a *public* limited company if the other shareholders agree
13. A person you owe money to
14. The shares in a *private* limited company can be bought and sold freely
15. Another name for a business
16. When a limited company fails, it goes into *liquidation*
17. Money you owe to another person
18. Shares in public limited companies are usually bought and sold at a . . . . . . exchange (which is also called a . . . . . . market)

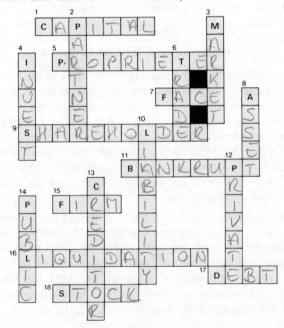

Exercise 10.5   Types of business

Complete this table about the four main kinds of business in Britain taking your information from the text in Exercise 10.4.

TYPE OF BUSINESS	NUMBER OF OWNERS	NAME OF OWNER(S)	LIABILITY OF OWNER(S)	IF THE BUSINESS FAILS . . .	ADDITIONAL INFORMATION
Sole proprietorship	*1* a	*proprietor* b	unlimited	owners go *bankrupt*	
partner-ship d	*2-20* e	Partners		c	
private limited company f	2-50	*shareholder* g	*limited by shares* h	company goes *liquidation* i	Name of company includes word <u>Limited</u> or abbreviation Ltd. Shares sold privately with agreement of other shareholders. Must have <u>Memorandum of Association</u> and <u>Articles of Association</u>
PLC j	2 or more				Name of company includes words Public Limited Company or abbreviation plc. Shares sold _____ k

Exercise 10.6   Must/can

Complete the following sentences with *must* or *can*. Take your information from Exercises 10.4 and 10.5.

1 There . . . . . . be at least two partners in a partnership.
2 A person who wants to start a business, but who has not got any partners . . . . . . start a sole proprietorship.
3 Two people starting a business together . . . . . . start a partnership or a private limited company.
4 You . . . . . . have as many as 20 people in a partnership.
5 A sole proprietor . . . . . . pay the firm's debts with his/her own money if necessary.
6 Each partner . . . . . . pay the firm's debts with his/her own money if necessary.
7 Anyone . . . . . . buy shares in a public limited company.
8 The name of a private limited company . . . . . . include the word *limited* or the abbreviation *Ltd.*
9 You . . . . . . only buy shares in a private limited company if the other shareholders agree.
10 You . . . . . . draw up a Memorandum and Articles of Association when you start a limited company.

Exercise 10.7   *Unlikely possibilities*

In pairs, discuss unlikely possibilities, like this:

P: *If you buy shares, you'll own part of the company.*
R: *I'm not going to buy shares.*
P: *But if you bought shares, you'd own part of the company.*

1   If you start a business, you'll need capital.
2   If the bank gives you a loan, you'll pay interest on it.
3   You'll have unlimited liability if you start a partnership.
4   If you buy shares, you'll be a shareholder.
5   You'll be a partner if you invest in a partnership.
6   If the limited company fails, you'll only lose the value of your shares.
7   If you buy a controlling interest, it'll cost you several thousand pounds.

> *Laboratory drill A*
> P: If you buy shares, you'll own part of the company.
> R: *I'm not going to buy shares.*
> *Laboratory drill B*
> P: If you buy shares, you'll own part of the company.
> R: *If you bought shares, you'd own part of the company.*

Exercise 10.8   *Problem-solving*

Decide what sort of business you would start in these situations. There is no one correct answer in any case and you may be able to think of more than one possibility. Give reasons for the decisions you make.

1   You and your spouse (husband or wife) want to start a grocery shop in a small village. There is already one grocery shop in the village owned by an old lady. Your bank will lend you the money you need.
2   Two couples have enough money to buy a small hotel which they will all work in. One of the couples has two young children.
3   You want to sell fruit and vegetables from a stall at the market. You need £500 capital which you can borrow from your father.

Exercise 10.9   *A Memorandum of Association*

In order to start a limited company, you must draw up two legal documents, a Memorandum of Association and the Articles of Association. In small groups, start your own company. Decide on the name of the company, what you are going to do and how much capital you are each going to invest. Then draw up the Memorandum. Write a full sentence for each of the six clauses, which say the following:

1   The name of the company (*The name of the company will be . . .*)
2   The country where the company is
3   The type of trade the company will carry on
4   A sentence saying that the liability of the shareholders is limited by the amount invested in shares in the company.
5   The amount of capital the company has and the number and value of its shares.

6 A sentence saying that the shareholders wish to form this company. Each shareholder signs the Memorandum and writes next to his/her name the number of shares he/she is buying. Write the date.

NB   The Articles are more complicated and give details of how the company will be run, how often shareholders' meetings will be held etc. Do not write this document.

Exercise 10.10   *Describing a graph*

Describe what happened to Transworld's share prices over the last twelve months, like this:

P: *Did share prices rise (go up) in January?*
R: *No. They fell (went down) sharply by 35 points.*
P: *Did share prices remain stable in February?*
R: *No. They rose (went up) slightly to 70.*

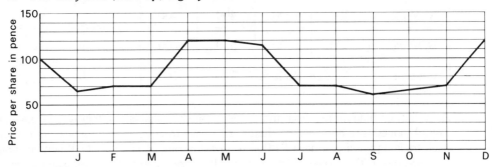

Laboratory drill
P: Did share prices fall in January?   R: *Yes. They went down sharply.*

Exercise 10.11   *Graphs*

Work in groups of four. Each student copies a different one of these graphs. Without showing anyone else your graph, describe it to people from other groups, until you have found all the other people in the class with the same graph.

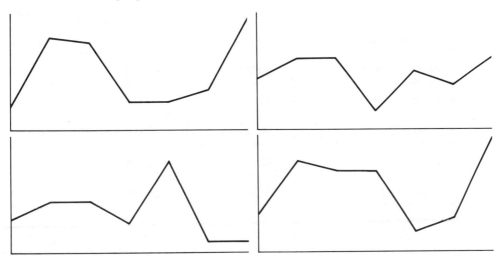

Unit 10

Exercise 10.12   *A simulation: Speculating*

 Here is what the share prices on the Stock Exchange have been for six companies over the past four trading periods:

TRADING PERIOD	1	2	3	4	5	6	7
ABC plc	250	200	200	125			
DEF plc	175	175	175	200			
GHI plc	200	225	220	250			
KLM plc	450	500	400	400			
NOP plc	620	900	500	200			
QRS plc	New co. No record.			100			

As well as earning money from the dividend on your shares, another way of making (or losing) money is to buy and sell shares. You have three chances to invest your money. In each trading period you have £1,000 to invest in one company only. When everyone in the class has written down which company they are going to invest in, play the tape to find out whether the share prices rose, fell or remained stable. Make a note of how much money you have won or lost. Invest another £1,000 for the next trading period, and so on. The winner is the person who makes the biggest profit over the three trading periods. Your record of your investment should look something like this (this is only an example):

TRADING PERIOD	5	6	7
COMPANY	CBA plc	TUV plc	XYZ plc
PRICE PER SHARE	100 pence	125 pence	250 pence
AMOUNT INVESTED	£1,000	£1,000	£1,000
NO. OF SHARES	1,000	800	400
NEW PRICE	50 pence	250 pence	250 pence
VALUE	£500	£2,000	£1,000
MADE (LOST)	(£500)	£1,000	—
RUNNING TOTAL PROFIT (LOSS)	(£500)	£500	£500

Language notes

Second conditional

We use the second conditional for present or future possibilities which are unlikely to happen. The *if* clause (*if* + subjunctive) and the main clause (*would* or modal verb + infinitive) can be in either order. The subjunctive is exactly the same as the past simple except in the verb *to be* when it is always *were*.

POSITIVE	*If I were rich, I could start a company.*
	You would lose your money if the company failed.
QUESTION	*What would you do if you were rich?*
	If your company failed, would you lose all your money?
NEGATIVE	*I wouldn't live here if I were rich.*
	If I weren't poor, I wouldn't live here.
SHORT ANSWER	*Yes I would. No he wouldn't.*

Modal verbs: must/can

MUST/HAVE TO/HAVE GOT TO express obligation (see Unit 12 for the negative)

PRESENT	FUTURE	PAST
I must go now.	*We will have to leave.*	*We had to leave.*
He has to leave soon.		
They have got to stay here.		

CAN expresses ability or possibility

PRESENT	FUTURE	PAST
He can type.	*He will be able to type*	*He wasn't able to type*
He is able to type.	*when he has done the*	*before the course.*
	typing course.	*He could speak French.*
We can go now.	*We can leave at about 6.*	*He couldn't leave then.*

Fractions

$\frac{1}{5}$	*a fifth*	$12\frac{1}{4}$	*twelve and a quarter*
$\frac{4}{5}$	*four fifths*	$33\frac{1}{3}$	*thirty-three and a third*
$\frac{7}{8}$	*seven eighths*	$66\frac{2}{3}$	*sixty-six and two thirds*
$\frac{1}{2}$	*a half*	$18\frac{3}{4}$	*eighteen and three quarters*

British English	American English
Banks do not pay interest on *current accounts* in Britain (account holders can pay by *cheque*). Banks pay interest on *deposit accounts*, which are designed for people to save money.	Account holders of *checking accounts* can pay by *check*. They save money in a *savings account*.
When a limited company sells its assets to pay its debts it *goes into liquidation*. When private individuals or partnerships do the same, they *go bankrupt*.	When companies or private individuals sell their assets to pay their debts, they *go bankrupt* or *go into bankruptcy*.

Consolidation B
Transworld News

TRANSWORLD NEWS

What's in my diary for today?

9.30 dictation; 10.30 manager's meeting; 12. lunch with Mr Fletcher, 2pm ask me to retype your letters without mistakes; 2.30 work on your report; 3.30 correct my typing again; 3.50 sign your letters even with mistakes; 4pm go home in a bad temper again.

Do you know?
Do you know which countries these are the capitals of? You should if you are in freight forwarding!

Helsinki – Riyadh – Lima – Athens – Vienna – Brussels – Tokyo – Washington DC – Cairo – Edinburgh – Stockholm – Moscow – Canberra – Warsaw – Rome

A MESSAGE FROM THE COMPUTER

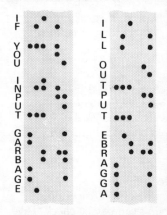

PUNCTUATION IS UNNECESSARY – OR IS IT?

To save time and to make life easier we leave out most punctuation in the headings and endings of modern business letters. However, in the body of the letter punctuation makes the message clear. For example, which of these firms is talking about more than one customer?

a) All our customers' goods . . .
b) All our customer's goods . . .

And can you punctuate this sentence so that it makes sense?

there is too much space between stars and and and and and stripes

Does it help if I tell you that the speaker is talking to someone who is painting a sign for a restaurant called 'The Stars and Stripes'?

And finally can you punctuate this sentence in another way so the boss is wrong?

'The secretary,' said the boss, 'is wrong.'

Business News in Brief

1. Internal Airways have improved their domestic service *and* brought down their prices. IA now have regular flights between ten cities in this country and their fares are about the same as first class rail fares. Airfreight rates are lower too.

2. The government have announced Newpoundland's trade figures – the Balance of Trade is in the red, but our Balance of Payments is in the black. The trade deficit is £1.2 m, but because of the large number of visitors to Newpoundland this year, our Balance of Payments surplus is just over two million pounds.

3. The pound is standing strong against the dollar at 2.56. Last month the pound was only worth $2.1. As a result we expect to handle more exports than imports in the next few months.

4. We regret to announce that one of our customers has gone into liquidation. ABD plc was a building firm which worked mainly on private housing. About two thousand ABD workers are now unemployed.

5. The major credit card companies say that they lose about £3,000,000 a year in this country from stolen cards. The figure in Dollardy is three times that amount. The latest figures show that one in six people now hold at least one credit card and that 90% of credit card holders have two or more cards.

6. The Stock Exchange closed at 254.3 on the last day of the month. This is 5.4 points down on the previous month, but 10.2 points up on the same month last year.

The editor invites you to write an article or send in jokes, cartoons on any items you think will interest other Transworld readers.

Exercise B   Business News

 Read 'Business News in Brief' and then listen to the 'Business News Headlines' on the tape.

1 Which 'News in Brief' item contains an error?
2 Which 'News in Brief' item is not on the tape?
3 Which taped news item is missing from 'News in Brief'?
4 Put the 'News in Brief' items in the order you hear them on the tape.
5 Which taped News Headline item contains an error?

Unit Eleven
Airfreight

 Jane Long is on the phone arranging an airfreight consignment with British Airways.

Jane Long here from Transworld. I'd like to arrange a consignment to Rome as soon as possible.

1

Oh. Then it'll have to be tomorrow. What time's the flight?

2

Leaves Manchester eleven o'clock ...arrives 14.40. And what's the flight number?

3

4

BA/AZ892. Thanks very much.

5

Yes I have. Do you want the number?

6

It's 125-4828 63740.

Unit 11

Exercise 11.1   A telephone conversation

From the pictures on the previous page, write the other half of the telephone conversation you think Jane has. Then listen to the tape and discuss any differences between the tape and what you have written.

Exercise 11.2   An air waybill

Give short answers to these questions about the air waybill opposite.

1   Which company is selling the goods? BOS LTD
2   Which company is buying the goods? CASOLO - GINELLI SPA
3   Which airport are the goods leaving from? Manchester
4   Which airport are they going to? Milan
5   How many boxes are the goods in? 3
6   What is the total volume of the boxes? 4,5 m³
7   How much does each box weigh? 120K
8   There are different markings on each of the boxes. What are they? Bos/cas. GIN / M
9   How many copies of the waybill are there? 3
10   Is this the top copy? No it isn't
11   What currency is used in the waybill? pound sterling
12   What is the cost per kilo to send the goods by air? £ 2,065
13   What are the other charges for? due carrier + due agent
14   How much must the buyer pay when the goods arrive? Nothing

Exercise 11.3   Listening for differences

Listen to the tape of Jane arranging an airfreight consignment and see how many differences you can find between that consignment and the one in the air waybill opposite.

Exercise 11.4   Synonyms

Which words on the left are synonyms of (mean the same as) which words on the right?

1   air waybill   h
2   buyer   d
3   exporter   f
4   airline   a
5   charge   g
6   description   i
7   measurements   e
8   box   c
9   original   b

   a   carrier
   b   top copy
   c   case
   d   consignee
   e   dimensions
   f   shipper
   g   rate
   h   air consignment note
   i   nature

Exercise 11.5   Arranging a consignment

In pairs, act out a telephone conversation as if you were Jane and the airline clerk. Arrange to send the consignment in the air waybill opposite. The flight leaves at 10.35 and arrives in Milan at 13.45 local time.

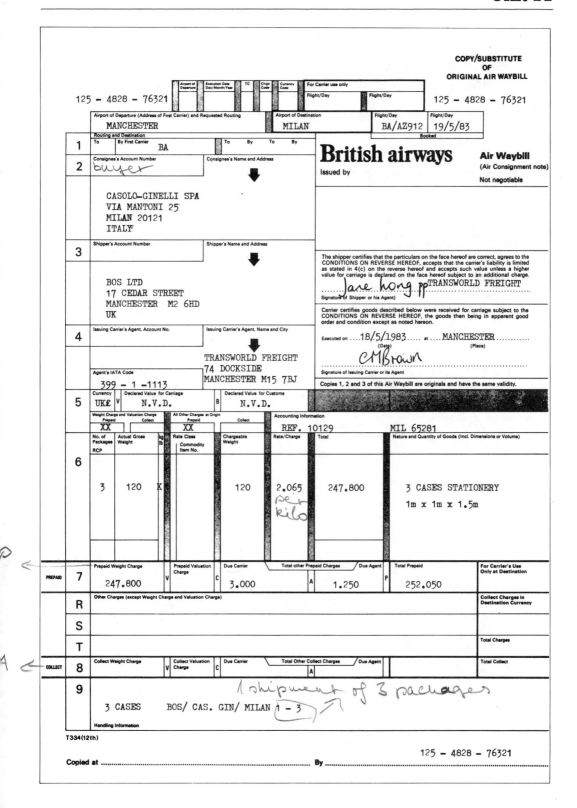

Unit 11

Exercise 11.6 *Deduction: might be/can't be/must be*

Work in pairs. One student covers the 'information' section on the flight board. Discuss who is on which flight. Your conversation will be something like this:

P: *What about this one? He says his flight leaves at half past three.*
R: *He might be on AQ942 or on GC387.*
P: *No he can't be on AQ942 because it's cancelled.*
R: *Oh. So he must be on GC387.*

INTERNATIONAL DEPARTURES			
FLIGHT NO	DESTINATION	DEPARTS	INFORMATION
ZR 506	CAIRO	14.45	DELAYED ONE HOUR
LP 193	NAIROBI	15.00	CLOSED
MX 251	ATHENS	15.15	BOARDING GATE 15
BJ 863	TOKYO	15.20	BOARDING GATE 4
EN 274	GENEVA	15.25	
AQ 942	BRUSSELS	15.30	CANCELLED
GC 387	DELHI	15.30	

Laboratory drill A
P: I hope it's warm in Nairobi.   R: *He says he hopes it's warm in Nairobi.*

Laboratory drill B
P: I hope it's warm in Nairobi.   R: *He must be on LP193.*

Exercise 11.7 *A mix-up*

Transworld are sending four different consignments to companies in four different countries by four different means of transport. Unfortunately all the papers are muddled up. From this information, can you work out what is going where by which means of transport?

Work in pairs and discuss your ideas as you work through the information, like this:

P: *Oh, so ADP can't be in France.*
R: *No. And GBD must be importing shoes.*

COMPANY	ADP			
COUNTRY				
CONSIGNMENT	furniture	cutlery		
MEANS OF TRANSPORT		train		

1 ADP is importing furniture.
2 The company which is importing stationery is in France.
3 The cutlery is travelling by train.
4 The Greek company is called GBD.
5 The ship is going to Spain.
6 The Italian company is called XLN.
7 The shoes are being flown to Greece.
8 The trailer is delivering goods to TJM.

Exercise 11.8 *Telex abbreviations*

Luigi Casolo-Ginelli started writing this letter to Geoffrey Best at BOS Ltd:

```
I was delighted with the first order of stationery (reference

MIL 65281) and I would like to order more. I would be grateful

if you could despatch a repeat order as soon as possible.

Could you also please tell me whether you could offer a

discount on bulk purchases?
```

He then decided he wanted an answer quickly, so this is the telex he sent and the answer he received:

```
BOS 660831 G
CASGIN 625037 I MILAN 14/6/1983 1045

ATTN BEST

DELIGHTED FIRST ORDER YR STATIONERY REF MIL65281
AND WANT MORE.  PLS DESPATCH RPT ORDER SOONEST.
CLD U OFFER DISCOUNT ON  BULK PURCHASES?+

REGARDS
CASOLO-GINELLI


CASGIN 625037 I
BOS 660831 G
```

```
CASGIN 625037 I
BOS 660831 G   MANCHESTER 14/6/83 1315

ATTN CASOLO-GINELLI

DELIGHTED STATINREXXXX STATIONERY OK. RPT ORDER
FOLLOWS. ADVISE FIVE PERCENT DISCOUNT ORDERS OVER
THREE HUNDRED STERLING PAYMENT  WITHIN SIXTY DAYS,
REGRET NO DISCOUNT UNDER THREE HUNDRED+

REGARDS BEST


BOS 660831 G
CASGIN 625037 I
```

In pairs, discuss the abbreviations used in telexes, like this:

P: *What does SOONEST mean?*
R: *I think it means 'as soon as possible'.*

1	ATTN	5	U
2	REF	6	CLD
3	PLS	7	YR
4	RPT	8	OK

Exercise 11.9 *Discussing meaning*

Discuss the meaning of these words, like this:

P: *What do you think 'delighted' means?*
R: *I think it means 'very pleased'.*

DELIGHTED	(a)	very pleased	(b)	very sorry
DESPATCH	(a)	write	(b)	send
BULK	(a)	a small quantity	(b)	a large quantity
PURCHASES	(a)	things you buy	(b)	people who sell
ADVISE	(a)	want	(b)	tell
STERLING	(a)	pounds	(b)	dollars
REGRET	(a)	pleased	(b)	sorry

Laboratory drill
P: What do you think 'delighted' means?   R: *I think it means 'very pleased'.*

Exercise 11.10 *Writing telex messages*

Can you improve these five telex messages by

a   using abbreviations where possible
b   using single words instead of longer phrases
c   cutting out some short words such as articles (*the/a*), pronouns (*you/we*), verb *to be*, some prepositions (*in/on*)

Make sure your message can still be understood.

1   I HAVE RECEIVED YOUR TELEX ADVISING US OF THE ARRIVAL OF OUR CONSIGNMENT (ORDER NUMBER 11135). I AM SORRY TO TELL YOU THAT THE AIRWAYBILL NUMBER WAS NOT GIVEN. I WOULD BE GRATEFUL IF YOU COULD ADVISE US OF IT AS SOON AS POSSIBLE

2   WE WOULD BE GRATEFUL IF YOU WOULD SEND US FIVE HUNDRED TYPEWRITER RIBBONS REFERENCE 752 AS AN URGENT ORDER NUMBER 009182 AND QUOTE US THE PRICE AND DISCOUNT YOU WILL GIVE US

3   WE ARE ADVISING YOU OF THE ARRIVAL OF OUR AGENT IN HAMBURG ON THE 16TH OF JUNE. WE WOULD BE GRATEFUL IF YOU COULD CONTACT HIM AT THE INTERNATIONAL HOTEL

4   WE ARE VERY SORRY TO TELL YOU THAT YOUR CONSIGNMENT OF OFFICE CHAIRS (ORDER NUMBER 76529) HAS BEEN DELAYED FOR FOUR DAYS. IT IS NOW ARRIVING IN BILBAO ON THE 23RD OF JUNE

5   YOUR ORDER NUMBER 82310 IS READY FOR DESPATCH. WE ARE SORRY THAT YOUR PACKING INSTRUCTIONS HAVE NOT BEEN RECEIVED YET. WE WOULD BE GRATEFUL IF YOU WOULD ADVISE US OF YOUR REQUIREMENTS AS SOON AS POSSIBLE

Exercise 11.11 *A telex*

Write the telex Jane Long sent to Casolo-Ginelli about the arrival by air of the consignment of stationery mentioned in Exercises 11.1 and 11.5. Casolo-Ginelli's telex number is in Exercise 11.8. Transworld's is on page 77.

Unit 11

Exercise 11.12   *Vocabulary development*

Complete these sentences with nouns made from the verbs in brackets. The nouns are all in the puzzle, where a number always stands for the same letter, for example, 8 stands for E.

1   Please send us your packing (instruct).
2   The goods are ready for (despatch).
3   We will send you a letter of (confirm).
4   We must receive your (pay) immediately.
5   We are advising you of the (arrive) of our agent.
6   The (depart) of the ship is delayed.
7   We are sending you a (consign) of shoes.
8   Could you give me some (advise) about documentation?
9   Please tell us your (require) immediately.
10   Here's the money. Can I have a (receive) please?
11   Could you give me a (quote) for shipping the goods?
12   Can you arrange the (transport) of goods to France?
13   Do you give a discount on bulk (purchase)?
14   Which (fly) are you on?

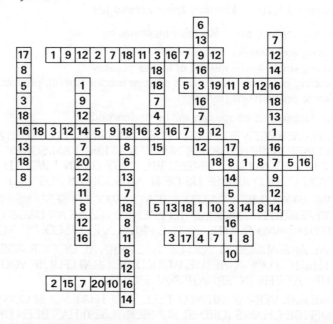

Language notes

Modal verbs: might be/can't be/must be

MUST BE expresses a logical deduction (ie the only possible reason for something)
You're wet. It must be raining.
Her name is Mrs Norman. She must be married.
CAN'T BE expresses a logical negative deduction (it is the negative of *must be*)
Her name is Miss Bell. She can't be married.
MIGHT BE expresses logical deduction when there is more than one possibility
Her name is Ms Long. She might be married or she might be single.

Unit Twelve
Import Regulations

 Nick Dawson is talking to Sandra Parr at Transworld.

Nick, what's a bonded warehouse?

Well, importers usually have to pay duty when they import goods.

That's at the customs, isn't it?

That's right.

When the importer doesn't pay the duty immediately, the goods are stored in a bonded warehouse.

So you can't take them out of the bonded warehouse until you pay the duty.

That's right.

I see. Thanks.

Any time.

Unit 12

Exercise 12.1   *Listening comprehension*

Listen to the tape and decide which word has which meaning:

1 Duty *g i c*
2 Warehouse *f*
3 Customs official *e*
4 Tariffs *g*
5 Bonded warehouse *a*

6 Declare *d*
7 Storage charges *b*

a Building where imported goods are stored until the duty is paid
b Cost of keeping the goods in a warehouse
c Another word for *tariff*
d Say what goods you are importing
e Person who collects the duty on imported goods
f Building where goods are stored
g Money paid to the government on imported goods

Exercise 12.2   *Definitions*

Rewrite these definitions and say which words they define, like this:

Goods are stored in this building.
A *building where goods are stored is called a warehouse.*
This document is used when goods are sent by air.
A *document which is used when goods are sent by air is called an air waybill or an air consignment note.*
This person collects duty on imported goods.
A *person who collects duty on imported goods is called a customs official.*

1 Goods are stored in this building until the duty is paid.
2 This money is paid to the government on imported goods.
3 This person imports goods.
4 This document is used for sending goods by sea.
5 Goods are produced in this building.
6 This person sells goods abroad.
7 This company arranges transportation and documentation.
8 These goods are being sent by sea.
9 Goods are being sent to this place.
10 Goods are loaded on to ships in this place.

Exercise 12.3   *Import regulations*

ALAND $250	BELAND $175	CELAND $275	Key
			$000 Cost of manufacturing one motorbike
			Market for motorbikes (each symbol represents 10,000 bikes sold per year)
			Coast

Aland, Beland and Celand all manufacture motorbikes. The biggest market for motorbikes is in Aland, so both Beland and Celand export to Aland. It is cheaper to manufacture motorbikes in Beland than in Aland, so the Beland bikes could sell at a cheaper price. However, the Aland government wants to protect its own manufacturers, so it has imposed import restrictions. The first restriction is that only a certain number of motorbikes may be imported into Aland each year, so anyone who wants to import motorbikes must have an import licence (permission to import).

The second regulation is that importers of motorbikes manufactured in Beland must pay import duty on them. There is no duty on bikes manufactured in Celand. When motorbikes arrive in Aland from abroad, the importer fills in a customs entry form giving details of the goods and where they are coming from. These details must be the same as the details on the commercial invoice. (This is the name of an invoice for imported goods. The commercial invoice may contain charges for transport and insurance as well as giving details of the goods and price like an invoice for the domestic market.) The Customs officials use the details on the commercial invoice to calculate the duty.

When goods are imported from Beland, the Customs officials want to be sure that the details on the commercial invoice are correct. When motorbikes are imported from Beland, a special commercial invoice must be signed by a representative of Aland's government who lives in Beland. This person is called the consul and the special invoice is called a consular invoice.

Goods from Celand have to travel through Beland to reach Aland. All motorbikes from Celand have a Certificate of Origin to prove that they have come from Celand.

Take your information from the text and write notes to replace the numbers to complete this flow chart:

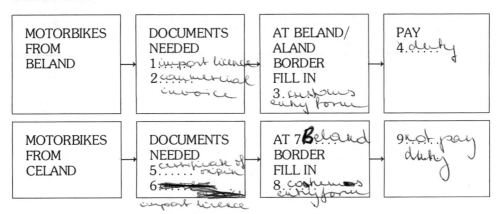

Exercise 12.4 *Reading comprehension*

Give short answers to these questions about the text in Exercise 12.3.
1 Which countries manufacture motorbikes? A, B, C
2 Where is the biggest market for motorbikes? in A
3 How much does it cost to manufacture motorbikes in each country? A-250, B-175, C-275
4 Do Aland motorbike manufacturers need an import licence to sell bikes in Aland? No
5 Who needs an import licence? A's importers
6 Which document must every importer fill in? customs entry form
7 On which country's motorbikes do importers have to pay duty? Beland
8 Why don't importers have to pay duty on Celand's bikes? more expensive than A
9 Why do importers need a Certificate of Origin for bikes manufactured in Celand? ?
10 Would importers want a Certificate of Origin for bikes manufactured in Beland? No

So they would have to pay duties

Unit 12

Exercise 12.5   *Customs documentation*

What do you think these documents are called?

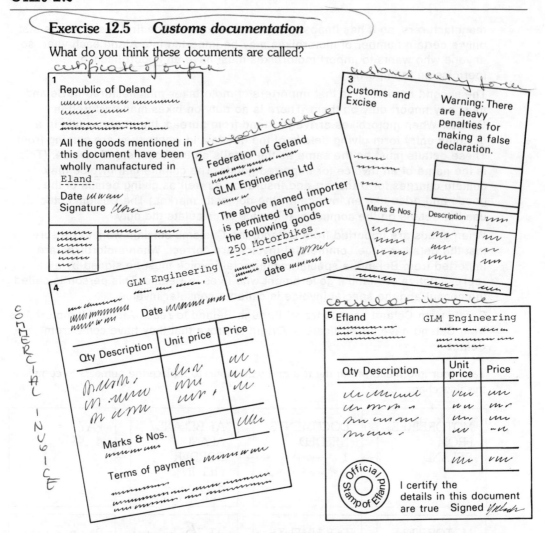

Prepare a short talk (about a minute) on what each document is used for. In small groups, take it in turns to name another student and say which document he/she should talk about.

Write a paragraph describing the use of two of the documents.

Exercise 12.6   *Obligation*

Complete these sentences with *must*, *do not have to* or *must not*.

1 Importers ...... declare goods at Customs.
2 Importers ...... import motorbikes into Aland without an import licence.
3 Aland importers ...... pay duty on motorbikes from Celand.
4 Importers ...... write false information on the customs entry form.
5 Goods from Celand...... travel through Beland to reach Aland.
6 Motorbikes from Beland ...... have a Certificate of Origin.
7 Aland importers ...... pay duty on motorbikes from Beland.
8 Consular invoices ...... be signed by the consul of the importing country.

Which sentences can you rewrite using *have to*?

Exercise 12.7   *Having things done*

This is a list of things which need doing at Transworld. Decide whether you will do them yourself or whether you want someone else to do them. Discuss the list in pairs, like this:

P: *I must mend the photocopier.*
R: *That'll keep you busy.*
P: *I must have the photocopier mended.*
R: *Who will you get to do it?*

---

1. mend the photocopier

2. check the consignment

3. send out the invoices

4. clean all the typewriters

5. collect the import licences

6. sign the forms

7. type the reports

8. copy the documents

Laboratory drill A
P: I must mend the photocopier.
R: *That'll keep you busy.*
P: I must have the photocopier mended.
R: *Who will you get to do it?*

Laboratory drill B
P: The photocopier's broken.
R: *I must have it mended.*

Exercise 12.8   *A consignment*

Hidden in this puzzle are eight documents which might be involved in sending a consignment abroad by trailer. What are they? Each number always stands for the same letter, eg 1 = C

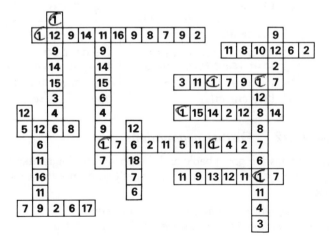

1 C.... O.... O....
2 C.... E.... F....
3 I.... L....
4 O....

5 C.... N....
6 I.... C....
7 C.... I....
8 C.... I....

Unit 12

Exercise 12.9   *Note-taking*

Listen to the short talk on the tape about the Customs and complete these notes. One word is missing from each gap. Don't try to write down everything the lecturer says. Just fill in the missing words.

CUSTOMS AND EXCISE

Representatives of a country's ¹*government*

Found at ²*ports* and ³*airports*

Four main functions:
- to ⁴...*calculate*... and collect ⁵...*the duty*... on imported goods (only dutiable goods)
- to issue ⁶...*import licences*... and export licences for restricted goods
- to prevent ⁸*trade* in forbidden goods
- to collect ⁹...*import*... and ¹⁰...*export*... figures

Use figures to ¹¹...*calculate*... the country's ¹²*Balance* of *Trade*

Exercise 12.10   *The function of the Customs*

Use your notes from Exercise 12.9 to write a paragraph about the Customs. Your paragraph will be shorter than the talk you listened to. You should not repeat things.

Exercise 12.11   *Negotiations*

The government representatives of Aland and Beland are negotiating trade agreements. They each have five points for negotiation.

In pairs, suggest possible solutions, like this:

ALAND: *If you buy our butter, we'll buy your cars.*
BELAND: *Or else if you buy our cars, we won't export tea.*

We want Beland to buy our butter.

We don't want Beland to export tea.

We don't want Beland to charge duty on apples.

We don't want Beland to increase their tariffs.

We want Beland to buy our oil.

We want Aland to buy our cars.

We want Aland to import our wool.

We don't want Aland to impose tariffs on cars.

We don't want Aland to impose import restrictions.

We want Aland to buy our shoes.

Exercise 12.12   *Further negotiations*

Your negotiations are going badly and the possibility of agreement is less and less likely. Try negotiating again, but this time show that you do not think the possibility is very great, like this:

Aland: *If you bought our butter, we'd buy your cars.*
Beland: *Or if you bought our cars, we wouldn't export tea.*

Laboratory drill
P: If you buy our butter, well buy your cars.
R: *If you bought our butter, we'd buy your cars.*

Exercise 12.13   *A simulation: Trade negotiations*

This chart shows what six countries produce and how much it costs them. It also shows what there is a market for in each country.

EMLAND Produces: *Motorbikes* ($250 unit price) *Shoes* ($5 unit price) *Tea* ($60 tonne) Market for: **Motorbikes** **Butter** **Tea**	ARLAND Produces: *Wool* ($120 tonne) *Motorbikes* ($200 unit price) *Cars* ($400 unit price) Market for: **Tea** **Cars** **Wool**	TELAND Produces: *Cars* ($350 unit price) *Butter* ($60 tonne) *Shoes* ($6 unit price) Market for: **Shoes** **Wool** **Butter**
OLAND Produces: *Motorbikes* ($300 unit price) *Wool* ($100 tonne) *Tea* ($40 tonne) Market for: **Shoes** **Wool** **Motorbikes**	VELAND Produces: *Tea* ($50 tonne) *Shoes* ($7 unit price) *Butter* ($40 tonne) Market for: **Tea** **Cars** **Shoes**	ESSLAND Produces: *Wool* ($80 tonne) *Cars* ($450 unit price) *Butter* ($50 tonne) Market for: **Butter** **Motorbikes** **Cars**

Divide into six groups, one group to be the government of each country. You have ten minutes to have a government meeting to consider the following questions:

1   What do you produce? Which markets (domestic and/or export) do you want to sell to?
2   Look at your own market. What do you want to import? Do you want to pay a lot or a little for imports? Which countries do you want to import from?
3   Do you want to protect any of your producers? How can you do that? If you impose a tariff, how much will it be? (eg If you manufacture typewriters at $100 each and your competitors make them for $80, what will a reasonable tariff be?)
4   Are there any countries you want to make trade agreements with?

You now have ten minutes to negotiate with other countries if necessary and to draw up and sign any agreements.

You have a further five minutes to make a final decision about any trade restrictions you want to impose. Write down your trade restrictions. One representative of your government must go to an international conference and make a formal announcement of your country's trade policy.

After the simulation, discuss the policies of each government. Did they make the right decisions? Why do countries trade with one another?

Unit 12

Unit Thirteen
Quotations

 An American importer, Jack Hyam, is dictating a letter to his secretary, Polly Ware.

1 Take a letter please, Polly.

2 'Dear Chris. It was nice...' — Could you speak a little more slowly please?

3 'Could you give me two quotes... the first FOB Liverpool...' — Pardon?

4 FOB. You write the letters FOB. No, no. In capitals.

5 'Yours truly' etc etc. — Yours truly what?

6 Ah, Polly? Are you sure you're happy in this job?

Exercise 13.1 *Listening comprehension*

Listen to the tape and give short answers to these questions:

1 Had Jack and Chris met before they saw each other at the trade fair?
2 Where was the trade fair?
3 How many times has Jack been to England?
4 Has Jack bought this tartan cloth before?
5 Is this tartan cloth already sold in America?
6 How did Polly write 'FOB' at first?
7 Has Chris ever been to New York?
8 On Jack's business card below what does 'Jr' stand for?

Exercise 13.2 *Dictation*

Listen to the tape and write the letter Jack dictates to Polly. These are the business cards of Jack and the person he is writing to:

MILLCO Ltd.

THE MILLS
RIVER STREET
HALIFAX HX5 7PT

Christopher Faram

Tel: Halifax (STD 0422) 9786430
Telegrams/cables: MILLCO HALIFAX

HOUSE OF HYAM Inc.
511 Free Street
New York NY17211

Jack Hyam Jr
SALES DIRECTOR

Tel: (212) 8756985
Telex 23150639 VW
Cables HYAMINC NEW YORK

Exercise 13.3 *Intonation*

Listen to Chris Faram dictating a letter to his secretary. When you hear a BLEEP on the tape, decide whether he has finished his sentence (his voice goes down) or whether he is going to add something (his voice is rising), like this:

P: The address is 511 Free Street, New
   York   R: *Finished*
P: The address is River Street, Halifax   R: *Not finished*

1 Thank you for your letter
2 We would like to order some desks
3 Could you give me quotations for 300 standard desks
4 The first is FOB New York and the second C&F Liverpool
5 Could you also give me quotations for 20 executive chairs
6 The first is FOB New York and the second C&F Liverpool
7 I look forward to hearing from you
8 Please give my regards to your wife

Laboratory drill
P: The address is Ilford Road, York   R: *Not finished*

Exercise 13.4   *Abbreviations*

Which five terms used in quotations are represented by these initials?
FOR, FOB, FAS, C&F, CIF
The words are all in this box.

Free	Alongside	Freight
	On	Ship
Cost	Insurance	Rail
	And	Board

Exercise 13.5

When an exporter quotes a price for goods, the price may include some or all of the costs of transporting the goods to the importer. The exporter uses an abbreviation after the price to show what is included, eg £500 FOB.

Draw a chart like the one above. The list in the first column shows all the costs of sending a consignment of tartan cloth from Chris Faram's factory in Halifax to Jack Hyam's warehouse in New York. Fill in a tick on your chart for things you think are included in each price abbreviation and put a cross if you think things are not included. For example, a price *franco* (which means *free*) includes the price of the goods and packing, plus all transportation and insurance to the importer's warehouse. The price *ex works* (out of the factory) only includes the cost of the goods and the packing. The first column is filled in for you.

What is included in the price?	Costs	Ex Works	FOR	FAS	FOB Liverpool	C+F New York	CIF New York	FRANCO 511 Free Street New York
1) Goods		✓						
2) Packing		✓						
3) Rail transport		×						
4) Loading charges		×						
5) Seafreight		×						
6) Insurance		×						
7) Landing charges		×						
8) Customs duty		×						
9) Transport to importer		×						
Price charged								

Unit 13

Exercise 13.6   *Pricing an export consignment*

Listen to the tape and correct your answers to Exercise 13.5 if necessary. Then listen again and complete the costs in the second column of the chart on page 107.

Exercise 13.7   *Problem-solving*

1   Pretend you are Chris Faram, the exporter. Give seven price quotations for the tartan cloth, *ex works*, FOR, FAS etc.
2   The House of Hyam is a very large company which imports a lot of goods by sea, so the shipping company gives them a discount. Millco is only a small company and cannot get a discount on the seafreight. Do you think Jack Hyam will accept the FOB price or the C&F price?
3   Chris Faram is paying £100 for the insurance. If the exchange rate is £1 = $2, how much will he charge Jack Hyam for the insurance?
   If Jack Hyam insures the consignment in New York, he will pay $180. Will Jack accept the C&F price or the CIF price?
4   With all the knowledge you now have about this consignment, which price quotation do you think Jack Hyam will accept?
5   You want to import stereo equipment from the USA. You receive quotations from three different companies for exactly the same quality and quantity of goods. The quotations are (a) $1,000 FOB (b) $1,000 C&F (c) $1,000 ex works. Which quotation will you accept?

Exercise 13.8   *Deduction: can't have been/must have been*

Work out what the terms were for these consignments and write about them like this:

When BOS exported stationery, they paid all the costs to the importer's warehouse.
The terms can't have been ex works. They must have been franco.

1   When GLM imported motorbikes, they arranged all the costs of transportation and the insurance.
2   When Millco exported cloth to New York, they paid the transportation costs until the goods were on the ship. The importer arranged the seafreight and other payments.
3   When JLN imported goods, they did not arrange any transportation until the goods were at the port of arrival, but they paid the insurance premium themselves.
4   When FSX exported goods, they paid all the transportation costs until the goods were at the port of arrival. They also paid the insurance.
5   When PDT exported a consignment of cars, they paid for the cars to be put on a train, but that is all.
6   When Moore & Moore imported shoes, they had to arrange payment of all the costs from the port of departure, including loading the goods on to the ship.

NB   Remember that the terms only show who arranges the transportation and pays the shipping company. Importers always pay all the transportation and insurance costs, whether they pay the shipping company or whether they pay the exporter.

Laboratory drill A
P: Must've   R: *Must've*

Laboratory drill B
P: I think the terms were FOB.   R: *You're right. They must have been FOB.*
P: I don't think the terms were CIF.   R: *You're right. They can't have been CIF.*

Exercise 13.9 *Formal and informal letters*

Arrange the four letters below and on page 110 in order of formality. Which is the most formal and which is the least formal? One of them is a personal letter, not a business letter. Which one? Discuss in pairs, small groups or as a class the difference between personal and business letters. Discuss what makes a letter formal or informal. Why are some letters more formal than others?

HOUSEHOLD
DESIGNS & CO LTD

22 High Street Manchester M1 2BL

Tel: (061) 763 2555
Telex: 668542 HODES
Cables/telegrams: HODES MANCHESTER

Mr John Stevens
Export manager
Pugliese SpA
Via Sottoriva 9
37100 Verona
Italy

30 June 1983

Dear John

It was nice to see you at the trade fair. You're certainly producing some excellent furniture.

We are particularly interested in your range of bedroom furniture. We think it would sell well here. Could you send me complete details of your range and let me know what discounts you can offer?

Jane and I are both well and look forward to seeing you in the summer. We both send our love to Susan and the children.

Best wishes

Peter

Peter Long
Sales Manager

Fashion Imports (Pty) Ltd

PO Box 35
Melbourne
Australia

Millco Ltd
The Mills
River Street
Halifax HX5 7PT
UK

28 June 1983

Our ref: BA/ej

Dear Sirs

We are interested in placing an order for 500 metres of your tartan cloth (ref J203).

We would be grateful if you would send us a quotation FOB Liverpool.

We look forward to hearing from you.

Yours faithfully

B. Abbs

Brenda Abbs (Miss)
Buyer

Transworld GmbH

Hochstrasse 28
2000 Hamburg

Tel: 040–3368 34   Telex: 7204388 Cables: TRANSWORLD HAMBURG

4 July 1983

Dear Mike

It was very nice to see you at the conference last week.
I'm sorry we didn't have more time to talk.

I'll be in England next week and I'll be in Manchester
on Tuesday (12th), so perhaps we could meet for lunch?
I'll ring you at the weekend to make sure you're free.

I look forward to seeing you then.

All the best

Simon

DEREGNAUCOURT SARL

Place Clair Bois 34
Marseilles
France

TEL: 91–64–86   Cables: DEREGNAUCOURT MARSEILLES

Millco Ltd
The Mills
River Street
Halifax HX5 7PT   4 July 1983

Dear Mr Faram

I was delighted to meet you at the trade fair last week and I very
much liked the cloth you produce.

I would like to place an order. Could you please send me a quotation?

I look forward to hearing from you.

Yours sincerely

J. Dupont

Jeanette Dupont (Mrs)

Exercise 13.10   *Personal description*

Write a description of Jack Hyam from what you've learnt about him in this unit. You might find some of the expressions in the box below useful.

Exercise 13.11   *Imagining people*

Write a description of one of the people mentioned in the letters in Exercise 13.9 without giving the person's name or nationality. Take as much information as you can from the letters and make up any other appropriate details. Give your description to another student to guess which person you have described.

PHYSICAL DESCRIPTION:
            about 30/45/50
            tall/short/medium height
            fat/thin/plump/slim/well-built/medium build
            long/short/dark/fair/curly/straight hair/bald/balding
            moustache/beard
            wears glasses/suits/dresses informally

PERSONALITY:
            efficient/not very efficient/intelligent/not very clever
            patient/impatient/lazy/hard-working/experienced/inexperienced
            good/bad-tempered

PERSONAL DETAILS:
            wife/husband/family/child(ren)/daughter(s)/son(s)
            lives in large/small/flat/apartment/house/in the town/country
            hobbies: sports – football/baseball/cricket/golf/swimming
                          reading/gardening/walking

Language notes

Modals: must have been/can't have been

MUST HAVE BEEN expresses logical deduction about past events. It is the past of *must be* (see Unit 11 language notes).
CAN'T HAVE BEEN expresses negative logical deduction about past events. It is the past of *can't be* (see Unit 11 language notes).

British English	American English
A supplier *quotes* a price for goods or gives a *quotation*.	A supplier *quotes* a price for goods or gives a *quote*.
The past participle of *get* is *got*.	The past participle of *get* is *gotten*.
Additional information in a sentence is sometimes given in brackets.( ).	Additional information is sometimes given in parentheses.

NB   The terms, eg FOB, CIF, described in this unit have different meanings in American English

Unit Fourteen
Seafreight

 The pictures show different stages in the transportation of a consignment from the UK to Australia by sea. Payment is by Bill of Exchange. Only the first and last pictures are in the right order.

a 1.

b 5.

12.

c 7.

d 6.

9.

e 2.

f 4.

g

10.

h 8.

i 3.

j

Exercise 14.1   *Description*

Use these notes to describe what is happening in each picture, like this:

a   exporter in UK loads consignment on board ship and receives Bill of Lading
The exporter in the UK is loading a consignment on board ship and he is receiving the Bill of Lading.

b   importer pays money into bank in Australia which sends it to exporter's bank in UK
c   importer in Australia exchanges Bill of Lading for consignment
d   bank in Australia gives Bill of Lading and other shipping documents to importer
e   exporter writes Bill of Exchange
f   UK bank sends two bills and other documents to bank in Australia
g   bank in Australia sends accepted Bill of Exchange to exporter in UK
h   importer writes 'accepted' on Bill of Exchange and signs it
i   exporter gives two bills and other shipping documents to bank in UK
j   exporter exchanges Bill of Exchange for money at bank in UK

Exercise 14.2   *Listen and match*

There are two different procedures that can be followed when exported goods are paid for by Bill of Exchange. Decide which picture at the beginning of the unit you think corresponds to which number in this diagram. Some pictures appear twice in the diagram. Listen to the tape to check your decisions.

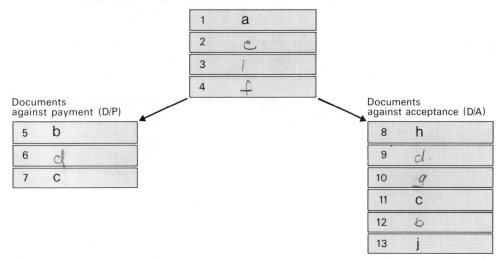

1	a
2	e
3	i
4	f

Documents against payment (D/P)

5	b
6	d
7	c

Documents against acceptance (D/A)

8	h
9	d.
10	g
11	c
12	b
13	j

Exercise 14.3   *A seafreight transaction*

1   GLM sent a consignment of micro-processors from Liverpool to BJT in Australia. The price was £1,000. BJT paid with a Bill of Exchange, D/P.

2   BOS London sent a consignment of stationery to DOM in Japan. The price was £750. DOM paid with a Bill of Exchange, D/A.

Write a description of these transactions as if you are the exporters and importers. In each case, describe the transaction which is better for you.

Start: (name of company) *loaded the* (type of goods) *on board ship in* (name of port) *and received the Bill of Lading. They then wrote the Bill of Exchange . . .* etc.

Or: *We loaded the* (type of goods) *on board ship in* (name of port) *and . . .* etc.

Unit 14

Exercise 14.4   *A Bill of Lading*

Decide which numbers these bits of information replace on the Bill of Lading opposite:

a 8 CASES MICRO-
   PROCESSORS
b GLM ENGINEERING LTD
   10 OAK WAY
   HALIFAX
c LIVERPOOL
d LIVERPOOL
e LIVERPOOL 19 July 1983
f THREE (3)

g MELBOURNE
h BJT (Pty)
   OUTBACK STREET
   MELBOURNE
i GLM/BJT MEL 1/8
j 139.2K
k X2053
l 1.16 cu.m
m 'AUSTRALIAN QUEEN'

Exercise 14.5   *Word puzzle*

Use the clues to help you fill in this vocabulary puzzle. All the words are taken from the Bill of Lading.

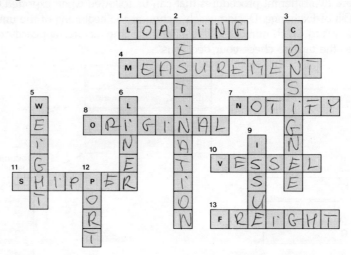

Clues
1 Putting goods on board ship   *loading*
2 The place things are going to   *destination*
3 The company the goods are going to   *consignee*
4 How big something is   *measurement*
5 How heavy something is   *weight*
6 A ship   *liner*
7 To tell   *notify*
8 A top copy   *original*
9 To write or give out   *issue*
10 A ship   *vessel*
11 The exporter, the company sending goods   *shipper*
12 A town on the coast where ships can visit   *port*
13 Goods; the cost of transporting goods   *freight*

114

LINER BILL OF LADING   B/L no.   2
TITAINER LINE

AUSTRALIAN SHIPPING SERVICE PTY
MELBOURNE – 25 KOALA STREET
TEL: 74245 TELEX: 15925 AA

SHIPPER	NUMBER OF ORIGINAL B/L
1 *consignor*	**4** *f*
	VESSEL 5 *m*
CONSIGNEE (IF 'ORDER' STATE NOTIFY PARTY)	**PORT OF LOADING** 6 *c*
ORDER	**PORT OF DESTINATION** *above* 7 *g*
NOTIFY PARTY *group of people* **3** *PTY (n)*	**FREIGHT PAYABLE AT** 8 *Liverpool*

MARKS & NOS	NO & KIND OF PACKING DESCRIPTION OF GOODS	GROSS WEIGHT IN KILOS	MEASUREMENT IN M^3
9	10	11	12
i	*a*	*j*	*l*

**FREIGHT PAID
IN LIVERPOOL**

Smith & Jones Co Ltd

Per *P. Jackson*

Place and date of issue
13 *c*

Signed (for the master) by

Smith & Jones Co Ltd
as agents *P. Jackson*

Unit 14

Exercise 14.6   *A Bill of Exchange*

A Bill of Exchange is a sort of post-dated cheque. Look at this Bill of Exchange and in pairs ask and answer questions about it, like this:

Ask who wrote the B/E.

P: *Who wrote the Bill of Exchange?*   R: *Sheila Baker*

Exchange for   *£ 750*   *London 14 July 1983*

At *90 days*   pay this   *solo*   Bill of Exchange

to the order of   *ourselves*

the sum of   *seven hundred and fifty pounds sterling*

Value   *goods*

To   *DOM KK.*   Signed   *Sheila Baker*
     705 3-chome Yamaguchi   For   *BOS Ltd*
     Osaka   *13 Mill Street*
     Japan   *Accepted*   *Harlow*
                  M Satsuma   *Essex CM20 2JR*
                  for DOM KK

---

1   Ask which company will receive the money. *BOS LTD*
2   Ask which company Sheila Baker works for. *BOS LTD*
3   Ask what date the Bill was written. *On the 14th of July*
4   Ask how much the Bill is for. *£ 750*
5   Ask how many copies of the Bill there are. *1*
6   Ask what date the Bill will be paid. *90 days after the 14th of*
7   Ask whether the Bill will be paid in pounds or in yen. *in pounds*
8   Ask which company will pay the Bill. *DOM KK*
9   Ask whether this transaction is 'documents against payment' or 'documents against acceptance'.
10   Ask who M Satsuma works for. *DOM KK*

Laboratory drill
P: Ask who wrote the Bill of Exchange.   R: *Who wrote the Bill of Exchange?*

Exercise 14.7   *Making out a Bill of Exchange*

Write a Bill of Exchange for the GLM-BJT consignment in Exercises 14.3 and 14.4. Think carefully what the differences will be between this and the B/E above. Some of the information is the same.

serve as a receipt for goods from ship

Exercise 14.8   *Negotiability*

proof of ownership

You already know two functions of a Bill of Lading. Its third function is as a document of title. A document of title is proof of ownership, so the person who owns the B/L may claim the goods. Look at the B/L in Exercise 14.4. Under the heading 'Consignee' is the word 'ORDER'. This word means that the B/L is negotiable – it can be sold. If you sell the goods you give the buyer the B/L so it can be used to claim the goods. The advantage of this is that the importer can sell the goods while the ship is still at sea. The buyer then presents the B/L and collects the goods when the ship arrives at the port of destination. The first importer has the money to start another transaction. This was very important when voyages took many months.

Credit is normal in export trade. When a B/E has been signed by the importer, the exporter usually has to wait about 90 (or sometimes 180) days before it can be exchanged for money. Because a B/E is negotiable, the exporter may discount (sell) the bill at his bank before the 90 days have passed. The exporter has the money to start another transaction immediately and the bank collects the money when the B/E is paid. The bank may rediscount the bill to a discount house which specialises in this work.

Give short answers to these questions about the passage:

1   What are the two functions of a B/L that you know already?
2   Which words on a cheque mean that it is negotiable?
3   Look at the air waybill in Exercise 11.2. Is it negotiable?
4   Do you think an exporter discounts a B/E when the transaction is 'documents against payment'?
5   When a bank discounts a B/E, do you think it pays (a) more than (b) the same amount as (c) less than the face value of the bill?

Exercise 14.9   *Word stress*

Decide where you think the main stress is in the words in italics and write them like this:
I want to *discount* the Bill of Exchange.   *dis – COUNT*

Then listen to the tape to check your answers.

1   A *Discount* House is a sort of bank.
2   Oil is an invisible *export*.
3   We want to *import* computers.
4   Did you *receive* the goods?
5   Could I have the *receipt* please?
6   My account is *overdrawn*.
7   I've got an *overdraft*.
8   What time does the plane *arrive*?
9   What is the time of *arrival*?
10 Which means of *transport* did you choose?
11 Did you *transport* the goods by train or trailer?
12 How much did the *transportation* cost?

Unit 14

Exercise 14.10   *Giving reasons*

Decide why Nigel Storke did the things on the left. His reasons are on the right (in the wrong order). In pairs, discuss what Nigel did and why, like this:

P: *Why did he go to the bank?*
R: *He went to the bank to cash a cheque.*

1 He went to the bank.
2 He rang the freight forwarders.
3 He went to the docks.
4 He flew to Amsterdam.
5 He picked up the phone.
6 He went to the telex room.
7 He sat down at his desk.
8 He went to the photocopier.

a He met the Dutch representative.
b He rang Transworld.
c *He cashed a cheque.*
d He sent a telex.
e He copied some documents.
f He arranged transportation.
g He wrote some letters.
h He delivered some freight.

Laboratory drill A
P: He went to the bank.

R: *Why did he go to the bank?*

Laboratory drill B
P: Why did he go to the bank?

R: *He went to the bank to cash a cheque.*

Exercise 14.11   *Definitions*

Write definitions of these words, like this:

INSURANCE CERTIFICATE: *It is a document which proves you are insured.*
VESSEL: *It is another name for a ship.*
BILL OF EXCHANGE: *It is a sort of post-dated cheque. You use it to pay for exported*
*   goods.*

BILL OF LADING; AIR WAYBILL; CONSIGNMENT NOTE; LINER; DIMENSIONS;
CREDIT CARD; BANKER'S CARD; COMMERCIAL INVOICE; CUSTOMS ENTRY
FORM; PROPOSAL FORM; STATEMENT; DOCUMENT OF TITLE

Read out one of your definitions to the class. Another student must guess which word you are defining.

Laboratory drill
P: I sent him the . . . you know, the consignment note for sending goods by sea. What's it called?
R: *Bill of Lading.*
P: That's right. I sent him the Bill of Lading.

118

Unit Fifteen
Letters of Credit

Kevin Hughes has just arrived back in the office at Transworld. He is talking to Sandra Parr.

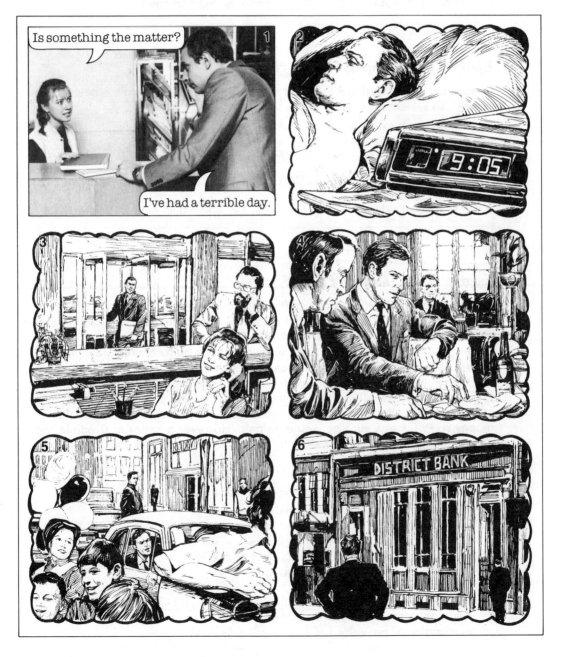

Unit 15

Exercise 15.1 *Listening comprehension*

Listen to the tape and give *Yes* or *No* answers to these pairs of questions:

1 Did Kevin's alarm clock go off? Did he wake up late?
2 Was he on time for work? Did Mr Storke arrive before him?
3 Did Mr Storke talk all morning? Did Kevin go to the bank before lunch?
4 Was the service in the restaurant slow? Did Kevin leave the restaurant before three o'clock?
5 Was there a procession? Did the traffic stop?
6 Did Kevin sit in a traffic jam? Did he get to the bank on time?

Exercise 15.2 *Impossible past conditions*

In pairs, talk about the things that went wrong with Kevin's day using the questions in Exercise 15.1, like this:

P: *Did his alarm clock go off?*
R: *No. That's why he woke up late.*
P: *Oh. So if it had gone off, he wouldn't have woken up late.*

> Laboratory drill
> P: . . . woken up late   R: . . . *woken up late*

Exercise 15.3 *Letters of Credit*

Bruce Stevens of Harbour Imports Pty, Melbourne, Australia, wanted to pay Peter Weaver of Clothco Ltd, Manchester, UK, for some cloth. Bruce wrote to his bank on a special form and asked them to open an irrevocable documentary credit. This is a Letter of Credit from Bruce's bank guaranteeing payment in Britain at a later date. If it is *irrevocable*, it cannot be cancelled. Neither Bruce nor his bank can change their minds and refuse to pay. Peter's bank knows Bruce's bank very well and they know they will receive the money, so they confirmed the Letter of Credit. This means that they guaranteed to pay the money so Peter was sure he would be paid. However a Letter of Credit is not negotiable, so Peter had to wait until the Letter of Credit was paid before he received his money.

Give short answers to these questions about the text:

1 Was Peter paid immediately for the cloth? No
2 Who applies for a L/C, the importer or the exporter?
3 Who issues a L/C? importer's bank
4 If a L/C is not irrevocable, who might not pay? the importer or his bank
5 If a L/C is not confirmed, who might not pay? the exporter's bank
6 Can you discount a L/C? it isn't negotiable
7 Do you think an exporter would rather be paid by B/E [D/P] or by L/C?
8 How many reasons can you think of why importers or banks might not pay a B/E or an unconfirmed revocable L/C? dishonesty
       financial failure

120 the currency might fail

Unit 15

Exercise 15.4 *Either/neither/both*

Complete these sentences with *either . . . or/neither . . . nor/both . . . and.*

1 If a L/C is irrevocable *either* the importer *or* his bank must pay.
2 If a L/C is irrevocable *neither* the importer *nor* his bank can refuse to pay.
3 B/E can be discounted *both* at a Discount House *and* at a bank.
4 A confirmed irrevocable L/C is guaranteed by *both* the importer's bank *and* the exporter's bank.
5 If a L/C is confirmed *neither* the importer's bank *nor* the exporter's bank can refuse to pay.
6 *Both* B/L *and* B/E are negotiable.
7 *Neither* air waybills *nor* L/C are negotiable.
8 If a L/C is unconfirmed and revocable *both* the importer's bank *and* the exporter's bank might refuse to pay.

Exercise 15.5 *Request to open a Letter of Credit*   *Bill of Lading*

Work in pairs with one student looking at this exercise and the other student looking at the request form on page 122. Ask and answer questions about the request form, like this:

Ask about the name of Bruce's bank.
P: *What's the name of Bruce's bank?*   R: *Old Australian Bank*
The student asking the questions should make a note of the answers. Change roles so the questioner gives the answers the second time. Are your answers the same?

1 Ask about the name of Clothco's bank. *Counts Bank plc. Manchester*
2 Ask about the date of the request. *29. July 1985*
3 Ask about the type of L/C Bruce wants. *irrevocable*
4 Ask about the beneficiary. *Clothco*
5 Ask about the amount. *£900*
6 Ask how long it is valid for. *90 days*
7 Ask about the number of documents required. *3 copies. B/L; import licence insurance certificate*
8 Ask about the kind of consignment note. *6 cases cloth*
9 Ask about the goods. ~~ASE~~
10 Ask about the unit price. *£150*
11 Ask about the terms.
12 Ask about the port of departure. *Melbourne*
13 Ask what is included in the price.
14 Ask which port Bruce would have written if the terms had been FOB.

> *Laboratory drill*
> P: What's the name of Bruce's bank?   R: *Old Australian Bank*

Exercise 15.6 *A Bill of Lading*

Draw the Bill of Lading that was sent with the consignment from Clothco to Harbour Imports. You can find most of the information you need in the Request to open a L/C on page 122.

121

application form

OLD AUSTRALIAN BANK Pty
INTERNATIONAL DIVISION
17 MAIN STREET
MELBOURNE

**REQUEST TO OPEN
DOCUMENTARY CREDIT**

Date 29 July 1983

Please open for my/our account a Documentary Credit, in accordance with the undermentioned particulars. Small print small print small print small. Print small print small print small print. Small print.

importer

Signed *Bruce Stevens*   Harbour Imports Pty, Billabong St., Melbourne

Entries must not be made in this margin	* Delete as necessary
Type of credit	*Irrevocable i.e. cannot be cancelled without beneficiary's agreement ~~*Revocable i.e. subject to cancellation~~
Method of advice	*airmail/~~cable~~
Advising bank	Counts Bank plc, Manchester, UK.
Name & address of beneficiary	Clothco Ltd , Cotton Lane, Manchester, UK.
Amount	£900 _say_ nine hundred pounds sterling
Availability	Valid until 31 October 1983 in Manchester for *~~acceptance~~/payment This credit is available by drafts drawn at 90 days sight/accompanied by the required documents
Documents required	Commercial invoice in three copies Full set Bills of Lading to order marked *freight paid/~~freight payable at destination~~ and 'Notify Harbour Imports Pty, Melbourne' ~~or~~ ~~Air consignment note~~ } ~~for goods addressed to~~ ~~Combined transport document~~ } ~~marked *Freights paid/freight payable at destination~~ Insurance certificate. Risks as follows: All Risks
Quantity & description of goods	Other documents: Import licence No LHDL 66 1983 6 cases cloth
Price per unit	£ 150
Terms & relevant port or place	*CIF, ~~C&F, FOB, FAS, FOR~~ etc. Melbourne
Dispatch/Shipment	From Liverpool to Melbourne
Documents to be presented	For *~~payment~~/acceptance within 14 days of the date of issue of the shipping documents
Special instructions	None

Exercise 15.7   *A Letter of Credit*

This is the Letter of Credit Bruce's bank issued for the consignment from Clothco. Unfortunately the bank clerk mixed up his request with another request. How many mistakes can you find in the L/C?

NAME OF ISSUING BANK	REVOCABLE DOCUMENTARY CREDIT
Old Australian Bank Pty International Division 17 Main Street Melbourne	Number 15927
Place and date of issue Melbourne, 1 August 1983	Place and date of expiry 30 September 1983 at counters of advising bank

Applicant   Clothco Ltd,
           Cotton Lane,
           Manchester, UK.
	Beneficiary
	Harbour Imports Pty
	Billabong Street
	Melbourne

Advising bank Ref no. Counts Bank plc Old Street Manchester	Amount £600 (six hundred pounds sterling)
Shipment/dispatch from Melbourne for transportation to Liverpool	Credit available with Counts Bank, Manchester By ☑ PAYMENT ☐ ACCEPTANCE against presentation of documents detailed herein and of your draft(s) at 90 days drawn on Harbour Imports Pty

Commercial Invoice in two copies.

Air Consignment Note for goods dispatched to Harbour Imports Pty Billabong Street, Melbourne marked 'Freight payable at destination'.

Insurance Certificate covering all Risks

Import Licence No. FNPJ 77 1983 covering 9 cartons cloth C & F Melbourne

Documents to be presented within 17 days after date of issue of shipping documents

We hereby issue this Documentary Credit in your favour. Small print. Small print small print small print small print. Small print small print small print. Small print small print

James Fletcher

pp Old Australian Bank Pty
   International Division
   17 Main Street
   Melbourne

This document consists of 1 signed page(s)

Unit 15

Exercise 15.8   *Vocabulary*

Use the clues to help you complete this puzzle. The words are all in the request form.

Clues
1 Another way of saying L/C
2 To cross out
3 To ask for
4 To send
5 The person the money is being paid to
6 The abbreviation is *no*
7 To issue a L/C is to . . . . . . a L/C
8 The exporter's bank is also called the . . . . . . bank
9 Legal, having value

Exercise 15.9   *Corrections*

Bruce wrote to the bank telling them of the mistakes in the L/C and giving them the correct information. Complete these sentences with *should have been* or *should not have been*, like this:

The L/C . . . . . . irrevocable.
The L/C should have been irrevocable. It should not have been revocable.

1 The date of expiry . . . . . . 30 September 1983.
2 The applicant . . . . . . Clothco Ltd.
3 The beneficiary . . . . . . Clothco Ltd.
4 The amount . . . . . .
5 The shipment . . . . . . despatched from Liverpool to Melbourne.
6 The shipping document . . . . . . an air consignment note.
7 The B/L . . . . . . marked 'Freight paid'.
8 The import licence number . . . . . .
9 The terms . . . . . . C&F.

Laboratory drill
P: The letter of credit was revocable.   R: *It shouldn't have been revocable.*
P: The letter of credit wasn't irrevocable.   R: *It should've been irrevocable.*

Exercise 15.10   *Comparisons*

In small groups, find as many similarities and differences between these pairs of documents as possible. A structure you might find useful is:

A B/L is a consignment note *and so is* an air waybill.
The importer's bank must pay a confirmed irrevocable L/C *and so must* the exporter's bank.

1   A cheque/a Bill of Exchange
2   A revocable documentary credit/a confirmed irrevocable Letter of Credit
3   A Bill of Lading/an air waybill
4   A Bill of Exchange/a Letter of Credit
5   An order/an invoice

Each student in the group should write a paragraph about a different pair of documents.

Exercise 15.11   *A letter of apology*

Write the letter of apology from Bruce's bank apologising for the mistakes in the L/C and enclosing the corrected L/C.·

Language notes

Third conditional

We use the third conditional about possibilities which did not happen in the past. The *if* clause (*if* + *had* + past participle) and the main clause (*would have* + past participle) can be in either order.

POSITIVE	*If you had been there, I would have seen you.*
	(You were not there – I did not see you)
	He would have done it if he had had time.
	(He did not do it – he did not have time)
QUESTION	*Would you have done it if I'd been there?*
	If you had seen him, what would you have done?
NEGATIVE	*I would not have done it if I had known.*
	(I did it – I didn't know)
	I would have done it if I had not seen you.
	(I did not do it – I saw you)
	I wouldn't have done it if I had not seen you.
	(I did it – I saw you)
SHORT ANSWER	*Yes I would. No he wouldn't.*

Should have

We use *should have* + past participle to express something which was not done or which was done wrongly in the past.

You should have written the letter. (I asked you to write a letter, but you didn't.)
You shouldn't have come home late. (I asked you to come home early, but you didn't.)

Consolidation C
Transworld News

TRANSWORLD NEWS

Dear Sir I enclose the invoice for a consignment of micro-computers which we are sending to New York by ship at the end of the month. I would be grateful if you could arrange insurance at your usual rate. I look forward to hearing from you in the near future. Yours faithfully etc etc. Have you got that?

Er... what came after 'Dear Sir'?

DO YOU KNOW?
Do you know what these abbreviations stand for? You should if you are in freight forwarding.
B/E FOR PLC B/L L/C
C&F A/C FAS

WHAT ARE THEY LIKE?
From the following information can you describe Ms U Scheidler and Mr S Birle, two of our Transworld personnel who work in the Hamburg branch? She is about 25, tall and slim and has long straight brown hair. He is about 30 and has short dark hair. The one with a beard also wears glasses. One dresses informally and the other usually wears a dress. Both are efficient, but the older one is more experienced than the one who cannot drive. One has a wife and two children and the other is unmarried. The family live in a house in the country and the single person lives in a flat in town. The one with curly hair likes playing football and tennis and also likes going to the theatre. The other spends a lot of time reading or at the cinema.

BUSINESS NEWS IN BRIEF

Transworld Manager Graham Davis holding the certificate for 'the company bringing the most credit to Manchester', which he received on behalf of his staff from the Mayor of Manchester.

From next January Transworld will use only the standard trade and shipping documents issued by SITPRO (Simplification of International Trade Procedures Board). We already use some of

their documents and as one of the major freight forwarders we feel we should support their efforts to simplify the procedures of international trade.

The Prime Minister is in Washington this week to talk to the President of the USA. They are discussing trade agreements between the two countries.

Mr John Smith is the winner of the 'Salesman of the Year' award for the second year running. Fifty-four-year-old John works for one of our customers – Smith Manufacturing plc (no relation to Smiths' Managing Director, Mr Frank Steele, said that he was delighted to have such an efficient representative on his staff. As a result of the award, John Smith will also receive a pay rise from the company.

Veland has imposed import restrictions on cars. In future, all importers must have an import licence and most countries will have to pay duty on imported cars.

ADVERTISING COMPETITION
As you all know our current advertising slogan is:–
TRANS port WORLD wide –
you can't forget the name!
Now we are looking for a new slogan. Have *you* got any ideas? We are offering a holiday for two in Las Palmas (you do *not* have to travel airfreight!) for (a) the best slogan (b) any slogan used to advertise the company. The competition is open to all employees of Transworld Freight plc or their subsidiary companies worldwide. Slogans before 31st December to Peter Murphy, London Head Office.

Exercise C *Business News*

With the help of the tapescript, complete the news items in 'Business News in Brief' where words have been left out through bad printing.

Export Mania

This is a board game for 2 to 6 players. All the players are car manufacturers who sell on their domestic market and export by sea to one other country:

Player A lives in Dollardy and exports to Newpoundland.
Player B lives in Dollardy and exports to Yenland.
Player C lives in Yenland and exports to Newpoundland.
Player D lives in Yenland and exports to Dollardy.
Player E lives in Newpoundland and exports to Yenland.
Player F lives in Newpoundland and exports to Dollardy.

Each player chooses a different exporter and plays with a different counter or coin. Throw a die in turns and move that number of squares. If you land on a square with writing, decide whether the information is important for your firm. If it is good news, move forward one square. If it is bad news, move backwards one square. If it makes no difference to you, stay where you are. If you move forward or backward on to a square with writing, you should also decide whether that information is important to you. You must reach the final square by throwing the correct number.

Start here by throwing die **1**	**2**	Yenland devalues its currency **3**	**4**	Newpoundland puts up its import duty **5**
16	World sales of cars fall **17**	The Dollardy government gives its car manufacturers a tax free allowance **18**	**19**	**6**
Newpoundland devalues its currency **15**	A ship sinks with some of your cars **24**	Congratulations you are named 'Exporter of the year' **25**	World steel prices rise **20**	Sea freight rates rise **7**
14	**23**	A new shipping company charges lower freight rates **22**	Your firm produces the world's best selling car **21**	A dock strike delays all goods coming into or going out of Dollardy **8**
Yenland imposes import restrictions on cars **13**	**12**	Dollardy lifts all import restrictions **11**	**10**	A rival company goes into liquidation **9**

Tapescript

Unit One

Exercise 1.1

AB: Hello. You're the new accounts clerk, aren't you? My name's Anne Bell. I do most of the secretarial work in the office.

DT: Pleased to meet you, Miss Bell. I'm David Thompson.

AB: Please call me Anne.

DT: And I'm David.

AB: Have you met anyone else yet?

DT: Only Liz, who works in the accounts department with me. Who is everyone?

AB: Well, the good-looking one over there, the one drinking now, is Kevin Hughes. He handles the exports.

DT: Who's he talking to?

AB: That's Jane Long. She arranges all our airfreight. The young man sitting at the table is Nick Dawson.

DT: The one eating a sandwich?

AB: That's right.

DT: What does he do?

AB: He spends a lot of time at the docks and the airport. He handles all the customs documentation.

DT: Oh, so Transworld handle documentation as well as transportation?

AB: Oh yes. And a lot of other things.

DT: And then I send the customers their bills.

AB: Yes. Come over here and let me introduce you to Sandra Parr. Sandra, this is David Thompson. David, this is Sandra.

DT: Hello, Sandra.

SP: Welcome to Transworld.

DT: Thanks.

AB: Sandra does all the important work in the office – the typing, the filing, the photocopying and so on.

DT: Oh, just the person I need. Could you show me how to work the photocopier please?

SP: Certainly. I'll show you straight after lunch.

Exercises 1.6 and 1.10

The tapescripts for these exercises are in the Teacher's Book.

Unit Two

Exercises 2.1 and 2.2

AB: Er . . . excuse me.

SA: I'm sorry. I didn't see you. Can I help you?

AB: Yes. I want to buy some crockery and cutlery for the office.

SA: Well this is our furniture department. Our range of crockery is over there. What exactly do you want?

AB Just cups, saucers and plates.

SA: I see. Well we have these plain dark blue ones or this pink flower design is very attractive.

AB: The dark blue ones, I think. How much are they?

SA: The small plates are £1.80 each, the cups are £1.90 and the saucers are £1.20.

AB: They're too expensive, I'm afraid. Have you got anything cheaper?

SA: Um . . . What about these with dark blue stripes? The plates and cups are 80p and the saucers are 60p

AB: That's quite cheap and they're very nice. I'd like twenty of each. Er . . . do you give a discount on that quantity?

SA: Yes. I can give you 10% on 20.

AB And can you deliver them? Our office is on Dockside.

SA: Yes. We'll bring them round this afternoon. Will that be all right?

AB: Fine.

SA: Now what about cutlery? It's over here.

AB: Something very simple. These plain ones will be fine.

SA: Certainly. What exactly do you need?

AB: Half a dozen knives and twenty teaspoons.

SA: Right. Six knives. That's £2.10. And 20 teaspoons. That's £3 for the teaspoons. There's no discount on those I'm afraid.

AB: That's all right.

SA: So your bill comes to er . . . £44.70 altogether. Will you pay in cash or by cheque?

AB: By cheque please. I've got a cheque card.

SA: That will be all right then. Make it out to Household Designs & Company Ltd please.

AB: Household Designs & Co Ltd. Forty-four pounds, seventy pence. There you are.

SA: Thank you.

AB: Could you give me a receipt please?

SA: Of course. Will the till receipt be all right or would you like a written one?

AB: A written one please.

Unit Three

Exercise 3.1

KH: Kevin Hughes speaking.

NS: Good afternoon. My name's Nigel Storke from GLM Engineering. I'm sending some machinery from Beeton to Norton and I'd like to discuss the best means of transportation. A friend told me the cheapest way is by sea.

KH: Well you can't send them directly from Beeton to Norton by sea. Norton isn't even on the coast.

NS: Oh. Beeton's on the coast though, isn't it?

KH: It is, but it hasn't got a port. There's a port at Easton, though, and you can send goods from Beeton to Easton by road or rail. They can travel from Easton to Sutton by ship and then you can either send them by trailer to Norton or by train via Ayton.

NS: And which of those is the best route?

KH: Well it depends how big your consignment is. It might be better to send the goods by air. There's an airport at Norton.

NS: And which airport do the goods travel from?

KH: The nearest airport to Beeton is at Weston. You'll have to transport the goods to Weston by road though. There used to be a railway line between Beeton and Weston, but there isn't any more.

NS: I see. Perhaps I'll send the details to you and you can arrange the cheapest route. Will you do that?

KH: That's what we're here for. I'd be delighted to help.

Exercise 3.12

Although containerisation has many advantages, it has some disadvantages too. And this is why many ports are still not specially adapted to container traffic.

Now, you need a lot of special equipment for handling containers and this is very expensive. Some countries haven't got enough money to buy the equipment to containerise their ports. Also – um – containerisation means that there is more unemployment, because the equipment does the work that people do in conventional ports. And most countries don't want a lot of people out of work, so they don't want their ports to be containerised.

Unit Four

Exercise 4.1

KJ: Welcome to 'Introduction to Business'. On today's programme we have David Constable, who is going to talk about insurance. David, when did insurance first start?

DC: The history of insurance in Britain is a long one. In the early days there was a lot of marine trade between Britain and India and America. So at that time, in the 16th century, people were insuring their cargo ships.

KJ: So the first kind of insurance was marine insurance? 1547

DC: Yes. Then in 1666 there was the Great Fire of London. Before then there were no fire brigades, but after the Great Fire insurance companies employed their own fire brigades to protect the buildings they insured.

KJ: How did people take out insurance?

DC: Well, the people who sell insurance are called underwriters, because they write their names under their promise to pay. In the 18th century, customers and underwriters used to arrange insurance in a coffee house which belonged to a man called Lloyd. Today Lloyd's is the name of a famous insurance market in London.

KJ: So if I want to insure a ship today, I must go to Lloyd's?

DC: No. You go to an insurance broker. The broker then goes to Lloyd's and arranges insurance for you with the underwriters who will give you the cheapest price.

Exercise 4.12

Use these clues to fill in the puzzle.

M: What's number one?

F: It's the people who put out fires. You know . . .

M: Oh yes. And number two?

F: Number two. Oh, it means something to do with the sea. It's a sort of insurance when you're insuring ships.

M: Uh-huh. And number three?

F: Those are the people who arrange insurance for other people.

M: Number four?

F: This word means a hundred years.

M: A hundred years. Oh, I know.

F: Number five means buildings or things you own.

M: Buildings or things you own. Mmmm. What about number six?

F: That means buying and selling. When you buy or sell things, you . . . . . .?

M: Oh yes. Seven?

F: These are the people who actually sell insurance. They promise to pay you if something goes wrong.

M: Uh-huh. Number eight?

F: This word means insurance. It's another word for protection or insurance.

M: Right. And the last one?

F: This is the money you pay for insurance.

M: Oh. Don't forget the hidden word.

F: Oh I think you know what that is now.

Tapescript

Unit Five

Exercise 5.1

SP: Sandra here.

LS: Oh hello, Sandra. It's Liz. Could I speak to Anne please?

SP: I'm afraid she's not here at the moment. Can I take a message?

LS: No. I'll ring her back later. . . . No I won't. Yes. Will you give her a message please? I've got an invoice here for some furniture from Household Designs, but I can't find the order. Does she . . .

SP: Oh wait a minute, Liz. She's just come in. Anne, it's Liz on the phone. She says she's got an invoice for some furniture from Household Designs, but she can't find the order.

AB: No that's right. I wrote a letter of order. I didn't send an order form.

SP: Liz? She says she wrote a letter of order. She didn't send an order form.

LS: Oh dear. We need an order number for our records. All right. I'll pay it.

SP: She says she needs an order number for the records, but she'll pay it.

AB: Er, can you also tell her that I bought some cutlery and crockery and I didn't use an official order.

SP: Liz?

LS: Yes?

SP: Anne says she bought some cutlery and crockery and she didn't use an official order.

AB: But I paid by cheque and I got a receipt.

SP: But she paid by cheque and she got a receipt.

LS: Yes I know. I've got the receipt. That's all right. Thanks a lot.

AB: What did she say?

SP: She said she'd got the receipt and that was all right.

Exercise 5.5

When you hear a BLEEP write (a) if the speaker means the listener and write (b) if the speaker means anybody in this situation.

1 I've sent you the invoice. BLEEP (You should have written a)

2 When you travel by train you need a ticket. BLEEP (You should have written b)

3 Next time you order goods, please use an official order form. BLEEP

4 To order goods you can send an order form. BLEEP

5 You don't receive many cheques from Germany. I don't think they use them. BLEEP

6 You haven't told me the invoice number. BLEEP

7 If you send goods by sea, you need a Bill of Lading. BLEEP

8 Which documents do you think were used? BLEEP

Consolidation A

This is Rosalind Foggin with Business News Headlines.

The price of oil is going up and so are freight charges. As a result, rail fares have risen by 2% and National Trailers say they are raising their prices next week.

Two new container ships are being built in Sutton Docks, which were containerised just a year ago. The cost of the ships is around £2m.

One of the big banks is going to charge its customers when they cash personal cheques. Counts Bank say there will be a charge of 50 pence per cheque. The other banks have decided not to charge any customers for this service.

The SS Titania picked up the crew of the Arctic Queen when she sank in the Indian Ocean. The disaster will cost Lloyd's underwriters about three million pounds.

A Belgian company has supplied West Trucks with twenty-six 'super-trailers' which go faster and carry heavier loads than most trailers used in this country. The Belgian company was not named.

And finally, a reminder from the post office to use the post code. Your letters will arrive more quickly if you do.

That's all from Business News Headlines. I'll be back with more news at 1 o'clock.

Unit Six

Exercise 6.1

KH: Hello, Sandra. Did anyone phone while I was out?

SP: Yes. I've taken these messages for you.

KH: Hmmm. Someone from Colourco wanting to know whether he can send a container to Turin by trailer. Yes he can.

SP: And that next one was somebody from Tanners, who asked whether we carry live animals.

KH: Well, I'm afraid I'll have to tell Miss Green that we don't handle live animals.

SP: This one is from Mr Black of Rainbow Co Ltd. He asked whether it was cheaper to send goods to Hamburg by road or rail.

KH: Well I can't tell him unless I know what the goods are. I'll ring him.

SP: I've answered these two, but I thought you'd want to see them. A Ms Brown asked whether we could collect goods from their factory. They're local, so I said we could. And another woman rang from Dyers. Her name's on the message. She wanted to know whether we handled containers.

KH: And you told her we did, I hope.

SP: Yes. And then Anne took this last one about European trailer rates. It was from a Mr Grey.

KH: Oh yes. He's from Spectrum. I'll give him a ring too. Thanks very much.

Exercise 6.4

F: Quick. Half a dozen people have asked me questions in the last few minutes. Can you write them down for me please before I forget? The first one wanted to know what time the flight to Germany was. The next one asked whether there was a flight from Hamburg to Manchester.

M: Just a minute. Say that again please?

F: Oh sorry. The second one asked whether there was a flight from Hamburg to Manchester. OK?

M: Yes. Next?

F: The third one asked how long the flight to Cairo took. How long the flight to Cairo took.

M: Got that.

F: The next one wanted to know whether there was a flight to Geneva on Sundays.

M: Whether there was a flight to Geneva on Sundays.

F: Next. A woman asked what time the Brussels flight arrived.

M: Uh-huh.

F: Then a man asked when the Paris flight left.

M: When the Paris flight left. Yes?

F: And the last one asked whether there was a morning flight to London. A morning flight to London.

M: Right. Shall I read those back?

F: Yes please.

M: One. What time is the flight to Germany? Two asked whether there was a flight from Hamburg to Manchester. The third asked how long the flight to Cairo took. The fourth asked whether there was a flight to Geneva on Sundays. The next one asked what time the Brussels flight arrived. Then a man asked when the Paris flight left and the last one wanted to know whether there was a morning flight to London.

F: Thanks very much. That's fine.

Unit Seven

Exercise 7.1

SP: Are those holiday brochures?

AB: Yes.

SP: What are you doing?

AB: Putting them in the wastepaper bin. I can't afford to go to the continent now.

SP: Why not?

AB: Look at this morning's paper. 'Pound weak'.

SP: How does the pound make a difference to your holiday?

AB: Well, if the pound's weak, you can't buy as much foreign currency. So things abroad are more expensive for the British.

SP: Oh I see. But inflation's making prices go up in Britain too.

AB: Yes, but there's inflation everywhere. This is different.

SP: Mmm. If the pound's weak though, more foreigners will buy British goods because they're cheaper. And that means the economy will improve. . . .

AB: And if the economy improves, the pound will be strong again.

SP: That's right. Get the brochures out of the bin! We can start planning next year's holiday.

Exercise 7.8

Country S spent £225,000 on computers and £200,000 on oil, so its total visible imports were £425,000.

It sold meat worth £300,000 to V and worth £100,000 to X, so its total visible exports were £400,000.

S spent £100,000 on tourism and £25,000 on insurance, so its invisible imports were £125,000. It has no invisible exports.

Country X spent £100,000 on meat and £300,000 on oil, so its visible imports were £400,000. X has no visible exports.

It spent £25,000 on insurance, so its invisible imports were £25,000. However tourists from V spent £100,000 and so did tourists from S. Tourists from Y spent £50,000 and tourists from W spent £300,000. X's total invisible exports, therefore, were £550,000.

Y spent £100,000 on computers and £100,000 on oil, so its visible imports were £200,000. It has no visible exports.

It spent £50,000 on tourism, so its invisible imports were £50,000.

It sold insurance worth £100,000 to V, worth £25,000 to S and worth £25,000 to X, so its invisible exports were £150,000.

W bought computers worth £600,000 from V and those were its only visible imports.

W exported £600,000 worth of oil to V, £200,000 worth to S, £300,000 worth to X and £100,000 worth to Y, so its total visible exports were £1,200,000 (that's twelve hundred thousand pounds).

Tourists from W spent £300,000 in X, which were W's only invisible imports. It has no invisible exports.

NB The summary of the figures is in the Teacher's Book.

Tapescript

Unit Eight

Exercise 8.1

AB: Oh no. This letter says I'm in the red.

SP: What?

AB: I've got an overdraft. My bank account's overdrawn. I've taken more money out of my account than I've paid in.

SP: Oh. What did you say the first time?

AB: I'm in the red.

SP: I haven't heard that expression before.

AB: It's because any amount that was overdrawn used to be written in red on your bank statement.

SP: That's interesting.

AB: Well anyway, I'll have to pay interest on the amount I'm overdrawn.

SP: Is that very expensive?

AB: Not usually as expensive as a loan, I suppose. And I can repay it when I get my pay cheque on Friday.

SP: Is there an expression that means you're not overdrawn? That your account is in credit?

AB: Yes. When you've got money in your account, the amount has always been written in black on your statement, so the expression is . . . . . .

Exercise 8.6

The tapescript for this exercise is the same as the exercise.

Unit Nine

Exercises 9.1 and 9.2

SP: Liz, this is ridiculous. I've just opened this letter and a customer's sent us a cheque for no pounds and no pence.

LS: What? Who?

SP: Someone from BOS Ltd. Listen to what he says. 'Thank you for your usual monthly statement. It says we have to pay you nothing. The one you sent last month said the same, so I now enclose our cheque for no pounds, no pence. Will this perhaps be the last time you send a statement of this kind? Yours faithfully.'

LS: Oh, we can thank the computer for that. All our accounts are computerised and it prints out a statement every month for our regular customers, even if they don't owe us money.

SP: Why do you send them?

LS: We don't usually, but David's new to the department and he probably sent it without even looking at it. I'll have a word with him about it. I'll also write a letter of apology to BOS.

Exercise 9.11

The tapescript for this exercise is in the Teacher's Book.

Unit Ten

Exercise 10.1

DT: Liz, who owns Transworld?

LS: I do.

DT: You? I don't believe you.

LS: Well, I own a bit of it. Transworld is a public limited company – that's what plc in the name stands for – and that means that anyone can buy shares in the company.

DT: And if you own shares, you own a bit of the company?

LS: That's right.

DT: Do all the shareholders work for the company?

LS: No. Most people invest in public companies to make a profit. It's like putting money in a bank deposit account where you earn interest.

DT: Do you earn interest on shares then?

LS: In a way. Except that the money you earn from shares is called a dividend.

DT: If you own a bit of the company, why are you an accounts clerk? Why aren't you the branch manager?

LS: Because it's a very big company and other people own more shares than I do.

DT: So if I bought more shares than you, I could have your job?

LS: You'd have to buy an awful lot of shares if you wanted to say which job you wanted. If you bought more than 50% of the shares, you'd control the company. Then you could do anything you wanted.

DT: Hmm. I could be the managing director.

LS: Before you get too excited . . . Have you got fifty thousand pounds or so?

DT: No. Why?

LS: Because that's what a controlling interest in Transworld would cost you.

Exercise 10.12

The tapescript for this exercise is in the Teacher's Book.

Consolidation B

This is Rosalind Foggin with Business News Headlines.

Newpoundland has a Balance of Payments surplus of £2.15m. This is mainly because of our invisible exports.

Interest rates are going up by 2%. This is bad news for savers, but good news for borrowers.

The Stock Exchange closed on the last day of the month at 254.3 after a poor month's trading.

A representative of a leading credit card company said that credit card companies in this country lose £3 million a year from lost and stolen credit cards.

Internal Airways have announced fare cuts of up to 10%. IA expect many more business people to use their service, particularly now they fly between ten major cities.

The pound is up 46 cents against the dollar compared to last month. Unfortunately this means we cannot expect as many tourists to visit the country this summer.

That is the end of Business News Headlines. We'll be back again at 6 o'clock this evening.

Unit Eleven

Exercises 11.1 and 11.3

BA:	British Airways airfreight. Good morning.
JL:	'Morning. Jane Long here from Transworld. I'd like to arrange a consignment to Rome as soon as possible.
BA:	To Rome. Just one moment. . . . Right. Well, you've just missed today's flight.
JL:	Oh. Then it'll have to be tomorrow. What time's the flight?
BA:	It leaves Manchester at eleven hundred and arrives in Rome at 14.40 local time.
JL:	Leaves Manchester eleven o'clock . . . arrives fourteen forty. And what's the flight number?
BA:	BA stroke AZ892.
JL:	BA/AZ892. Thanks very much.
BA:	Have you already filled in an air waybill?
JL:	Yes I have. Do you want the number?
BA:	Yes please.
JL:	It's 125 dash 4828 63740.
BA:	Right. That's 125–4848 63740. And how many cases are you sending?
JL:	Five. They're all one by one by nought point five.
BA:	Metres?
JL:	Oh. Yes.
BA:	And weight?
JL:	Total weight, one hundred and fifty kilos.
BA:	A hundred and fifty.
JL:	I'll send the cases up this afternoon, if that's all
BA:	That'll be fine. 'Bye.
JL:	Goodbye.

Unit Twelve

Exercise 12.1

SP:	Nick, what's a bonded warehouse? I know you store goods in a warehouse, but I don't know what 'bonded' means.
ND:	Well, importers usually have to pay duty to the government when they import goods.
SP:	That's at the customs, isn't it?
ND:	That's right. The importer declares the goods and the customs officials collect the duty.

SP:	Uh-huh.
ND:	When the importer doesn't pay the duty immediately, the goods are stored in a bonded warehouse.
SP:	So you can't take them out of the bonded warehouse until you pay the duty.
ND:	That's right. And the importer also has to pay storage charges – the cost of keeping the goods in the warehouse.
SP:	By the way, what's a tariff?
ND:	Oh, it's another word for duty.
SP:	I see. Thanks.
ND:	Any time.

Exercise 12.9

Listen to this talk and complete the notes in your book.

Er . . . now then. I'd like to tell you a bit about the Customs. Basically, the Customs, or Customs and Excise to give them their full title, are representatives of a country's government. They're a government department really. They're found at ports and airports . . . the places where people bring goods into the country. Now, they have four main functions. The first is to calculate and collect the duty on imported goods which are dutiable. You don't have to pay duty on all goods, remember. The second function is to issue import and export licences for restricted goods. To issue import and export licences for restricted goods. Three: To prevent trade in forbidden goods. That's to stop people trading in certain drugs, wildlife, that sort of thing. And their other, fourth function is to collect import and export figures. They use these figures to calculate the country's Balance of Trade.

So, remember their four main functions. One: to calculate and collect duty on imported goods (but only on dutiable goods). Two: to issue import and export licences for restricted goods. Three: to prevent trade in forbidden goods. And four: to collect import and export figures.

Now, are there any questions? . . .

Unit Thirteen

Exercises 13.1 and 13.2

JH:	Take a letter please, Polly. It's to Christopher Faram at Millco in England. The address is on his card here.
PW:	OK.
JH:	Now . . . 'Dear Chris. It was nice meeting you again at the trade fair.' Period. 'I always love . . .'
PW:	Ah . . . Could you speak a little more slowly please?
JH:	Sorry. How far have you gotten?
PW:	'Dear Chris.'
JH:	Ah. 'It was nice . . . meeting you again . . . at the trade fair . . . after such a long time.'

Tapescript

PW: '. . . meeting you again at the trade fair after such a long time.' Period. Yes?

JH: 'I always love . . . visiting your country.'

PW: 'I always love visiting your country.' Period?

JH: Period. 'Everyone back here . . . agrees with me . . . that your tartan cloth . . .'

PW: That your what cloth?

JH: Tartan. TARTAN. 'Everyone back here agrees with me that your tartan cloth would be very popular . . . in the US . . .' comma.

PW: '. . . would be very popular in the US . . .'

JH: '. . . so we would like . . . to place an order . . . as soon as possible.' Period.

PW: '. . . so we would like to place an order as soon as possible.'

JH: New paragraph. 'Could you give me . . . two quotes . . .'

PW: Two what?

JH: Quotes. 'Could you give me two quotes . . . for eight hundred meters of tartan cloth,' open parentheses, 'ref. J273,' close parentheses, comma . . .

PW: 'Ref. J273.'

JH: Now close parentheses. And put a comma. . . . 'the first FOB Liverpool . . .'

PW: Pardon?

JH: FOB. You write the letters FOB. No, no. In capitals.

PW: Like that?

JH: Yes. That's fine. Now where was I?

PW: 'Could you give me two quotes for eight hundred meters tartan cloth reference J273, the first FOB Liverpool . . .'

JH: OK. . . . 'and the second C and F New York.' You write that capital C, a plus sign for 'and', capital F. C and F New York. Period. New paragraph. 'I look forward to hearing from you . . .'

PW: 'I look forward to hearing from you . . .'

JH: '. . . and maybe to introducing you . . . to New York sometime.'

PW: '. . . to New York sometimes.'

JH: Not sometimes. Sometime. Period.

PW: OK.

JH: 'Yours truly' etc etc.

PW: Yours truly what?

JH: What?

PW: What comes after 'Yours truly'?

JH: My name – Jack Hyam Junior. And my position in the company. Do you know my position in the company?

PW: Sure. You're the Sales Director.

JH: That's right. Very good. Ah, Polly? Are you sure you're happy in this job?

Exercise 13.3

The tapescript is very similar to the exercise.

Exercise 13.6

When goods are sold *ex works*, the price includes only the cost of the goods and the packing. In the case of this consignment to New York, Chris Faram wanted to receive £2,000 for the cloth and the packing cost £150. The cost of transporting the goods to the railway station wasn't very much, so Chris didn't include this in the price. For this consignment, therefore, the *free on rail* price was the same as the *ex works* price. The cost of rail transport to the docks was £20. This was added to the FOR price for the *free alongside ship* price. For the FOB price, you must include the loading charges which were £25. The seafreight was £390. This is included in the *cost and freight* price. The CIF price is the same as the C&F price except that CIF also includes the insurance cost which was £100. The *franco* price covers all the costs of transporting the goods from Chris Faram's factory in Halifax to Jack Hyam's warehouse in New York. In this case, the landing charges were £40, the customs duty was £350 and the cost of transporting the goods to the House of Hyam was £25.

Unit Fourteen

Exercise 14.2

Listen to the tape and decide which picture corresponds to which number.

There are two ways a Bill of Exchange can be used to pay for goods sent by sea. The first is known as 'documents against payment' and the second 'documents against acceptance'. In both cases the first step is for the exporter to deliver goods on board ship and, in exchange, he receives the Bill of Lading from the shipping company. Secondly, the exporter writes the Bill of Exchange, which is a sort of cheque. Then the exporter takes the Bill of Lading, the Bill of Exchange and the other shipping documents to his bank. The bank sends the documents to the importer's bank.

When the procedure is 'documents against payment', the importer next goes to his bank in Australia. He pays the money which the Australian bank sends to the exporter's bank in the UK. In exchange the bank gives him the Bill of Lading and other documents. Finally, when the ship arrives at its destination, the importer gives the captain the Bill of Lading and receives the goods.

When the procedure is 'documents against acceptance', the first four stages are the same, but then the importer does not pay his bank the money for the goods. Instead he writes the word 'accepted' on the Bill of Exchange and signs it. This means he promises to pay the money at a later date – usually 90 or 180 days after the Bill is written. The bank then gives him the Bill of Lading and other documents. The importer's bank sends the accepted Bill of Exchange to the exporter, who now has proof that he will be paid in the future. When the ship arrives at its destination, the importer gives the captain of the ship the Bill of Lading and receives the goods. The importer then pays the money for the goods to his bank, which transfers it to the exporter's bank. The exporter can then exchange the accepted Bill of Exchange for the money.

Exercise 14.9

The tapescript is the same as the exercise.

Unit Fifteen

Exercise 15.1

KH: Sandra, can you remind me to go to the bank tomorrow morning?

SP: Certainly, Mr Hughes. Er . . . Is something the matter?

KH: I've had a terrible day. For a start, my alarm clock didn't go off, so I was late for work.

SP: Oh yes, I know. Mr Storke was here to see you.

KH: Humph. Well, he then talked all morning so I had to go straight from here to lunch with Geoffrey Best.

SP: Surely that was pleasant?

KH: Oh yes. Geoff's very nice. But the service in the restaurant was very slow. We didn't leave until after three o'clock. But then I'd forgotten about the procession.

SP: Procession?

KH: Yes. All the local schools have been having some sort of music festival.

SP: Oh yes. I remember.

KH: Well, anyway, the traffic couldn't move and I sat in a traffic jam for over half an hour. By the time I got to the bank it was closed.

SP: Well I'll remind you to go in the morning. Oh . . . and er . . . Mr Hughes?

KH: Yes?

SP: Don't forget to have your alarm clock mended.

KH: Oh right. Thanks.

Consolidation C

This is Rosalind Foggin with Business News Headlines.

This week the Prime Minister is in Washington with the US President discussing trade negotiations between the two countries.

In an effort to protect its own manufacturers, the Veland government has imposed import restrictions on cars. This means that all car importers must have an import licence and most countries – including our own – will have to pay duty on cars going into Veland.

The latest freight forwarding company to support the Simplification of International Trade Procedures Board. SITPRO, is Transworld Freight. SITPRO is working to simplify international trade procedures. Transworld say that from next January they will use only the standard shipping documents issued by SITPRO.

More news of Transworld – the mayor of Manchester has awarded them the prized certificate for the company bringing the most credit to the city. Transworld Manchester Branch Manager Graham Davis received the certificate on behalf of his staff.

And another prize winner – Mr John Smith who works for Smiths Manufacturing plc is the winner of the Salesman of the Year award for the second year running. Mr Frank Steele, Smith's Managing Director, said that he was delighted to have such an efficient representative on his staff. As a result of the award, Mr Smith will also receive a pay rise from the company.

And on that happy note I'll say goodbye. We'll be back with more Business News Headlines at 1 pm.

Word list

These are the commercial words used in this book. The number in brackets after each word is the unit in which it first appears.

AB (6)
a/c (2)
accepted (14)
account-holder (2)
accounts department (1)
advertisement (1)
advising bank (15)
air consignment note (5)
airfreight (1)
airport (1)
air waybill (5)
application form (1)
arrival (6)
Articles of Association (10)
AS (6)
assets (10)
assistant (2)
assistant manager (1)
balance (8)
Balance of Payments (7)
Balance of Trade (7)
bank (2)
bank account (2)
banker's card (2)
bankrupt (10)
B/E (14)
beneficiary (15)
bill (1)
Bill of Exchange (14)
Bill of Lading (5)
B/L (14)
board (11)
boarding gate (11)
bonded warehouse (12)
borrow (8)
branch (2)
brochure (7)
broker (4)
broker's slip (4)
bulk (6)
buy (2)
buyer (2)
C + F (13)
calculate (4)
calendar month (5)
caller (5)
cancel (11)
capital (8)
cargo (3)
carrier (11)
case (3)
cash (2)
central processing unit (9)
certificate of origin (12)
change (2)
charge by volume (3)
charge by weight (3)
cheque (2)
cheque card (2)
CIF (13)
claim (4)
clerk (1)
co (5)

combined transport document (5)
commercial invoice (12)
company (10)
compensation (4)
competitive (9)
complete (4)
component (6)
computer (6)
computer programmer (9)
confirmed (15)
consignee (11)
consignment (3)
consignment note (5)
consul (12)
consular invoice (12)
container (3)
containerisation (3)
controlling interest (10)
conventional cargo (3)
correspondence (1)
cost (2)
cost and freight (C + F) (13)
cost, insurance and freight (CIF) (13)
cover (4)
CPU (9)
credit (8)
credit card (8)
credit note (9)
creditor (8)
currency (7)
customer (1)
Customs and Excise (12)
customs clerk (1)
customs entry form (12)
customs official (1)
D/A (14)
damage (4)
data (9)
data processing (9)
debit note (9)
debt (8)
debtor (8)
declare (12)
deduct (4)
deficit (7)
delay (11)
deliver (2)
departure (3)
deposit account (10)
description (5)
despatch (11)
destination (3)
dimensions (3)
discount (2)
Discount House (14)
dispatch (11)
distribution (6)
dividend (10)
docks (1)
documentary credit (15)
documentation (1)
document of title (14)
documents against acceptance (14)

documents against payment (14)
domestic market (6)
D/P (14)
drawer (2)
duty (12)
economy (7)
effect (4)
electronic components (9)
employ (4)
employee (1)
endorse (2)
equipment (2)
exchange rate (7)
executive (13)
experience (1)
export (1)
exporter (6)
export manager (1)
extension (9)
ex works (13)
face value (10)
factory (6)
FAS (13)
favourable (7)
figures (7)
filing (1)
finance company (8)
finished goods (6)
firm (10)
flight (6)
FOB (13)
FOR (13)
forwarding agent (6)
franco (13)
free alongside ship (FAS) (13)
free on board (FOB) (13)
free on rail (FOR) (13)
freight (3)
freight forwarder (1)
freight rate (3)
GIGO (9)
GmbH (6)
goods (6)
graph (7)
guarantee card (2)
import (1)
importer (6)
import licence (12)
import regulations (12)
impose (12)
Inc (incorporated) (2)
inflation (7)
input (9)
insurance (4)
insurance certificate (4)
insurance company (4)
insurance market (4)
insure (4)
interest (8)
internal line (5)
in the black (8)
in the red (8)
invest (10)

136

investor (10)
invisible imports/exports (7)
invoice (5)
IOU (4)
irrevocable (15)
issue (14)
job (1)
Jr (13)
junior accounts clerk (1)
keyboard (9)
KK (6)
L/C (15)
lend (8)
Letter of Credit (15)
liability (10)
licence (12)
limited liability (10)
line (5)
liner (14)
Lloyd's (4)
load (3)
loan (8)
Ltd (2)
Ltda (6)
majority shareholder (10)
manufacturer (6)
marine (4)
market value (10)
means of transport (3)
measurement (3)
memo (1)
memorandum (1)
Memorandum of Association (10)
micro-chip (9)
nature (11)
negotiable (2)
negotiation (12)
no (5)
nominal value (10)
notify party (14)
NB (6)
office (2)
OK (11)
order (2)
original (11)
out-of-work (3)
output (9)
overdraft (8)
overdraw (8)
owe (8)
own (10)
pa (per annum) (8)
pack (3)
partner (10)
partnership (10)
par value (10)
pay (2)

payee (2)
per cent (5)
person Friday (1)
photocopy (1)
plc (5)
PLS (11)
port (3)
position (1)
post-date (2)
post-dated cheque (2)
premium (4)
price (2)
printer (9)
private limited company (10)
produce (6)
profit (10)
pro-forma invoice (5)
program (9)
property (4)
proposal form (4)
Pte Ltd (6)
Pty Ltd (6)
public limited company (10)
purchase (2)
put in (10)
qty (5)
quantity (5)
quotation (6)
quote (6)
rate (3)
raw material (6)
receipt (2)
ref (11)
reference (11)
regards (6)
reminder (9)
repay (8)
report (1)
retailer (6)
revocable (15)
RPT (14)
salary (1)
sales voucher (8)
SARL (6)
seafreight (1)
secretary (1)
seller (2)
senior accounts clerk (1)
services (7)
set up (10)
share (10)
shareholder (10)
shipper (11)
shipping documents (14)
shorthand (1)
signature (2)
small print (4)

sole proprietor (10)
sole proprietorship (10)
SOONEST (9)
SpA (6)
spend (2)
st (5)
statement (5)
stationery (2)
sterling (11)
Stock Exchange (10)
store (6)
submit (4)
subscription (8)
supplier (2)
surplus (7)
switchboard (1)
table (6)
tariff (12)
tel (5)
telex (6)
terminal (9)
terms (2)
ticket (5)
top copy (8)
trade (4)
trade figures (6)
trade negotiations (12)
trailer (3)
transaction (2)
transistor (6)
transport (3)
transportation (1)
travel and entertainment card (8)
type (1)
U (11)
undercharge (9)
underwriter (4)
unemployment (3)
unfavourable (7)
unit price (2)
unlimited liability (10)
unload (3)
valid (15)
value (6)
VDU (9)
vessel (4)
visible imports/exports (7)
visual display unit (9)
volume (3)
wages (3)
warehouse (6)
wholesaler (6)
working conditions (1)
YR (11)
Yours faithfully (1)
Yours sincerely (1)
Yours truly (1)

List of irregular verbs

INFINITIVE (present)	PAST SIMPLE	PAST PARTICIPLE
be (am/is/are)	was/were	been
bring	brought	brought
buy	bought	bought
choose	chose	chosen
come	came	come
cost	cost	cost
deal	dealt	dealt
do	did	done
draw	drew	drawn
drink	drank	drunk
eat	ate	eaten
find	found	found
get	got	got (UK)
		gotten (US)
give	gave	given
go	went	gone/been
grow	grew	grown
have/has	had	had
hear	heard	heard
keep	kept	kept
know	knew	known
leave	left	left
lend	lent	lent
make	made	made
meet	met	met
pay	paid	paid
put	put	put
read	read	read
ring	rang	rung
say	said	said
see	saw	seen
send	sent	sent
show	showed	shown
sink	sank	sunk
sit	sat	sat
spell	spelt (UK)	spelt (UK)
	spelled (US)	spelled (US)
spend	spent	spent
stand	stood	stood
steal	stole	stolen
take	took	taken
tell	told	told
think	thought	thought
understand	understood	understood
write	wrote	written